Photograph of Louis B. Mayer and 64 MGM stars for the Studio's 20th birthday, 1943

Left to right,
Front row:

James Stewart, Margaret Sullavan, Lucille Ball, Hedy Lamarr, Katharine Hepburn, Louis B. Mayer, Greer Garson, Irene Dunne, Susan Peters, Ginny Simms, Lionel Barrymore.

Second row:

Harry James, Brian Donlevy, Red Skelton, Mickey Rooney, William Powell, Wallace Beery, Spencer Tracy, Walter Pidgeon, Robert Taylor, Pierre Aumont, Lewis Stone, Gene Kelly, Jackie Jenkins.

Third row:

Tommy Dorsey, George Murphy, Jean Rogers, James Craig, Donna Reed, Van Johnson, Fay Bainter, Marsha Hunt, Ruth Hussey, Marjorie Main, Robert Benchley.

Fourth row:

Dame May Whitty, Reginald Owen, Keenan Wynn, Diana Lewis, Marilyn Maxwell, Esther Williams, Ann Richards, Martha Linden, Lee Bowman, Richard Carlson, Mary Astor.

Fifth row:

Blanche Ring, Sara Haden, Fay Holden, Bert Lahr, Frances Gifford, June Allyson, Richard Whorf, Frances Rafferty, Spring Byington, Connie Gilchrist, Gladys Cooper.

Sixth row:

Ben Blue, Chill Wills, Keye Luke, Barry Nelson, Desi Arnaz, Henry O'Neill, Bob Crosby, Rags Ragland.

THE MAN WHO SHOT GARBO

THE HOLLYWOOD PHOTOGRAPHS OF CLARENCE SINCLAIR BULL

TEXT BY TERENCE PEPPER AND JOHN KOBAL

Foreword by
Katharine Hepburn

Simon and Schuster

New York · London · Toronto · Sydney · Tokyo

In the preparation of this book and the accompanying exhibition,
the author has received considerable help and advice from a large number of people.
I am most grateful to Mrs Jeanne Bull for making available the invaluable research material
including Bull's own manuscripts that have formed the backbone of the text.
In New York I would like to thank the staff of the New York Public Library at the Lincoln Center
as well as Ben Carbonetto and Lou Valentino for the loan of valuable original Bull material
and in Los Angeles Robert Cushman of the Academy of Motion Picture Arts and Sciences
for his help with original negative material from the collection.
In London I should like to acknowledge the help of the British Film Institute Information Department
and Bridget Kinnally of the Stills Library and the American Embassy Information Library.
Simon Crocker, Jane Jacomb-Hood and Dave Kent of the Kobal Collection
have proved enthusiastic in their assistance.
Mark A. Vieira in San Francisco has generously supplied his personal recollections of Clarence Bull
as well as original material in his own collection. Peter Hall and Meribeth Bunch assisted me in Walton Street and
I am most grateful of all to John Kobal for offering his encyclopaedic knowledge and boundless enthusiasm
over a long period of time.
I should like to give special thanks to Ursula McMullan for her contribution,
Norman Kent for his quality printing and my colleagues at the National Portrait Gallery,
especially Gillian Forrester for her patient editing and general help.
Finally I should like to warmly thank Miss Katharine Hepburn for generously contributing
a lively foreword to the book.

Terence Pepper, April 1989
National Portrait Gallery

Simon and Schuster
Simon & Schuster Building
Rockefeller Center
1230 Avenue of the Americas
New York, New York 10020

First published in Great Britain by
Simon & Schuster Ltd.
West Garden Place
Kendal Street
London W2 2AQ

Simon & Schuster of Australia Pty. Ltd. Sydney

Printed in the Federal Republic of Germany
by Passavia, Passau

1   3   5   7   9   10   8   6   4   2

Library of Congress Cataloging in Publication Data
available upon request

British Library Cataloguing in Publication Data available upon request

ISBN: 0-671-69700-5

Contents

Foreword

Clarence Bull was one of the greats –
I was thrilled when I went to MGM to know that he was
going to photograph me. I was terrified –
Was I interesting enough?
He had done Garbo for years – The pictures
were extraordinary. Her head – his lighting –
they combined into something unique.
I felt like a sort of mouse – standing by
for a lion. He came – he was easy – he was sweet
– he was distant.
Listen – so was I – I was easy – I was
sweet – I was distant. We never got to know each
other – but I knew that he liked working with me –
and I knew that I liked working with him. In fact,
we were both delighted – we were relieved – we were
a happy pair and it was fun.
Now I can only say – Hey! Wasn't I lucky?
I sure was born at the right time.
Clarence Bull!
And the National Portrait Gallery!
WOW!

Katharine Hepburn
December 1988

Introduction

Terence Pepper

Hollywood in the 1920s and 1930s was the setting for a golden age of film productions. The major studios of the time such as Columbia, RKO, Universal, Paramount, United Artists, Warner Brothers and MGM competed to lure a willing public into their fantasy world of escapism, harnessing together a wide variety of creative talents to produce great motion pictures.

The most financially successful studio (and, by its own reckoning, artistically successful as well), and the one that employed the largest number of contracted stars was Metro-Goldwyn-Mayer. Led from its formation in 1924 by the paternalistic Louis B. Mayer, who was aided by the highly talented head of production, Irving Thalberg, the company boasted of its pre-eminence with the slogan, 'more stars than there are in Heaven'. Clarence Sinclair Bull worked on this Parnassus of glamour and commerce from its inception until his retirement in 1961 as the studio's chief portrait photographer. For almost forty years, as head of the Stills Department, Bull and the team of photographers he supervised produced icons of the age which fixed the studio and its stars in the public's imagination. Between 1918 and 1961 Bull himself photographed over 10,000 subjects and took over 4,000 individual studies of Greta Garbo. On his death in 1979 *Variety* paid tribute to Bull for his 'definitive portraits' of the galaxy of stars that he photographed. Many people would have been familiar with his images but few would have been aware that he was their author. Throughout the thirties Greta Garbo was arguably the most potent and memorable star of the period, attracting the largest cult following of any star of her era. From 1929 until her retirement from films in 1941 this most reclusive of stars would allow only Clarence Sinclair Bull to take her portraits. For each of her films she devoted one or two days to working in Bull's gallery and together they created magical and dreamlike photographs – the classic images of Hollywood portrait photography. This was one of the great collaborations of photographer and subject which compares with other great creative relationships in photography such as Arnold Genthe and Isadora Duncan, Alfred Stieglitz and Georgia O'Keeffe, Baron de Meyer and Nijinsky or Sir Cecil Beaton and the Royal Family.

The literature so far devoted to the history of motion pictures, film stars and directors is enormous but the number of books devoted to the artistry of the stills and studio portrait photographer is remarkably few. This literature includes partially ghostwritten autobiographies such as George Hurrell's *The Hurrell Style* (1977), and Bull's own book written with Raymond Lee, *Faces of Hollywood* (1968), an alphabetical arrangement of 250 of his portraits, interspersed with sections of short episodic text. Other monographs, such as John Engstead's *Star Shots* (1978) and Roman Freulich's *Forty Years in Hollywood: Portraits of a Golden Age* (1971), though written by or in collaboration with the photographer, are excessively modest in giving the men behind the camera their full due. Warner Brothers' production photographer Bert Longworth's *Hold Still Hollywood* (1937), an imaginatively designed book is a rare exception in illustrating the excitement and creative energy possessed by the talented photographers who were contracted to the studios and whose work was published, most frequently, then and now, anonymously. *Masters of Starlight* (1988) published to accompany a major exhibition at the Los Angeles County Museum of Art features 44 photographers out of an estimated 300 who worked in Hollywood between 1918 and 1973. It devotes brief biographies to each, and marks another important step forward in the re-evaluation of an art form that has exercised considerable influence on twentieth-century photographic portraiture. 'The Hollywood style', as this enormous body

9

of work is loosely called, has, after being unfashionable for a long period, staged a comeback in the revived careers of thirties and forties studio artists like George Hurrell, Laszlo Willinger, and Ted Allan; or in the work of young new photographers such as Herb Ritts, Matthew Rolston, Greg Gorman, and others who were promoted in the pages of Andy Warhol's monthly *Interview*. Warhol was a keen collector of the works of the Hollywood photographers and was influenced by them. (Warhol's close-up 'portraits' drew their original inspiration from the Hollywood close-up on still and screen. He used Bull's photograph of Garbo in her metallic head-dress for his screen-print definitive portrait of her.) The upsurge of interest can be closely linked to John Kobal's pioneering exhibition at the Victoria and Albert Museum, London, in 1974, and the accompanying book which grew out of the exhibition, which travelled throughout Europe, America and Australia, *The Art of the Great Hollywood Photographers* (1980). Also influential in the climate of general reappraisal of the golden age of the American cinema were such earlier works as *The Image Makers* (1972) and *Grand Illusions* (1973), two sumptuously illustrated books designed by Richard Lawton featuring Hollywood photographers at their best.

Shortly before his death Clarence Sinclair Bull was working with a long-time friend and editor of a photographic journal, Fred Schmidt, on a book of his memoirs. Sadly, only the early pre-Hollywood material was completed in any detail but I am extremely grateful to Mrs Jeanne Bull for allowing me to see this material, as well as her husband's early press cutting books and subsequent articles tracing his career from his formative beginning on a ranch in Montana. This archive was as valuable as it was unique. It is referred to in the text as *Unpublished Notes*.

Early Years

In *Faces of Hollywood* (1968), Clarence introduces himself in a chapter heading as a "Rawbone from Montana". All his life he was proud of his roots as one of the third generation of the Bull family to be associated with the town of Sun River. His grandfather, Charles Albert Bull Sr, had emigrated from Indiana and had opened a trading post there in 1867. Clarence's father,

Charles Albert Jr had been born in Sun River in 1874 and was educated there until his father, hoping that he would follow in the traditions of the eastern branch of the family which had produced several Judge Bulls, sent him to the University of Michigan to study law. There he met and married Belle Sinclair, a Scottish-Canadian school teacher from Chatham, Ontario. In 1894 he passed his bar exams for the Michigan Supreme Court with honours but instead of practising law, he returned home to Sun River with his wife. Clarence later commented that his father "was a born civil engineer and should have studied that" (*Unpublished Notes*). After an eventful journey West, the couple stayed on the Bull family ranch. Clarence was born on 23 May 1896.

After a short stint running the newspaper *The Sun River Sun*, Charles Jr, with two of his brothers, filed claims on adjacent homesteads. The young family moved into a house which he himself had built and, together Charles and Belle leased sufficient land to start a cattle raising business.

Belle entered with enthusiasm into her role as a rancher's wife, learning to ride, drive four horses and shoot. She used her teaching skills to tutor her son and each day time was set aside for his studies. By the time he was three he could read and, isolated as he was from the company of other children, he found companionship and entertainment in books. He also learned to ride bareback and on his sixth birthday was given his own horse and saddle. Most significantly of all for his future, when he was ten, he had his first introduction to the seemingly magical possibilities of photography.

"One summer, an aunt from Glendive (Montana) came to our ranch to visit us. She had a camera with her and took some pictures of the house, which had just been painted and still had some scaffolding standing against it. My aunt said not to worry. When the finished pictures came, there was no scaffold and most of the siding was hidden by a very strange shrub, the likes of which could not be found in Montana. I asked a lot of questions about that, but still didn't know what happened." Clarence was totally beguiled with the power of photography to transform a less than satisfactory reality into the ideal. "The magic involved in that picture sold me on photography" (*Unpublished Notes*). Unknown to Clarence, the 'magic' was in the retouching process and when he later took his own photograph of the same scene, he was much disappointed to find that the scaffolding obstinately remained in his picture to spoil the final result.

Clarence's interest in art was first stimulated by visiting the studio of the famous Montana cowboy artist, Charles Marion Russell (1868–1926). While still living on the ranch Clarence spent some time at the Columbus Hospital in Great Falls for a hip operation. Russell, the renowned painter of cowboys and western landscapes, was a friend of one of the nurses. Knowing of the boy's love of the popular artist's work, she arranged for Clarence to visit Russell's studio during his recuperation. Clarence was fascinated, visiting the studio many times, observing Russell at work on his sculptures, drawings and illustrations. Russell began to give him some lessons. "My fingers were sticks", Bull later wrote. "One day as I picked up a brush, he gently took it from me and said, 'Clarence, you're painting from your fingers. It must come from your heart. Now, I know you appreciate beauty and all that goes with it. Why don't you get yourself one of those Kodak cameras and let it exercise your fingers while you go to work on your heart!' As I trudged home through the snow I knew I had to get that Kodak or bust" (*Unpublished Notes*).

All had been going well with the Bulls' cattle business until May 1908, when a sudden blizzard struck and their cattle, penned temporarily (while waiting to be taken to the mountains for summer feeding), stampeded out of their enclosure and over a cliff edge. The family gave up the ranch and moved back to Sun River where Clarence's father went to work in a general hardware store. Clarence was 12 before he went to school for the first time and found himself, thanks to his mother's skilful teaching, well ahead of the others in his class.

Clarence, who had never forgotten his early enthusiasm for photography, devised various money-making schemes to save enough to buy a camera and keep himself supplied with film. After school hours he worked in his father's small grocery store and delivered copies of the *Saturday Evening Post* and other magazines on horseback to ranches in the area. He acquired a franchise to sell a line of corn cures, face creams and hair tonics. He sold Currier and Ives (prints of American scenes) to the local townspeople and ranchers. By the time he was 13, he had saved enough money to buy a Kodak film pack camera, a supply of developer (then sold in tablet form) and some Kodak Azo printing paper. He took pictures of western landscapes, towns, buildings, and action photographs of horses which he shrewdly marketed as postcards. He quickly began to make a small profit, enough to allow him to give up his other commercial activities, to the disappointment of some of his corn cure customers and the disapproval of his father who missed his help in the store.

In 1910 Clarence left Sun River to begin High School in Great Falls. His afternoons were free and he pursued his interest in photography and found a part-time job with the W. T. Ridgely Printing Company known mainly for its reproductions of Charles Russell's work. Clarence was fascinated by the printing process and took the opportunity to renew his acquaintance with Russell. This time he showed Russell some of his photographs. Everybody was happier. A long time later their paths crossed once more, when Clarence was in charge of the photo department of the Goldwyn studios and Russell was visiting his good friend, the celebrated cowboy philosopher and comic, Will Rogers. The photograph Bull took of the two men seated on Stage One of the lot was widely reproduced at the time (see illustration 1).

In 1914 he changed schools again and, staying with an aunt and uncle, moved to Port Huron where he found a part-time job in a camera store, which gave him the chance to learn about and experiment with the various makes available. He particularly liked the German Voigtländer and the English Ensign. Clarence also worked in the projection booth of a cinema and, because of his enthusiasm for photography, was soon appointed official High School photographer.

1 Will Rogers and Charles Marion Russell, 1922

2 Montana Bronco Buster, 1916

He was also given several photographic assignments through his work at the camera shop, photographing subjects as varied as ice breakers on Lake Huron and a local convention. He was especially proud of the natural unposed results he achieved in the finished work. When he was asked to photograph a semiprofessional stage play, he used a 4″ × 5″ camera with fast plates and no flash so that his pictures would be as unstilted as possible. He helped his subjects to hold still by asking them to count to themselves, a technique which was to prove useful again when in 1943 he had to photograph a group of 65 MGM stars for a celebrated colour feature on the American film industry in *Life* magazine.

Fascinated as always by the technical side of photography, Clarence, back at school, was allowed to use the laboratory facilities to experiment with his own research. He contacted Eastman Kodak about problems he encountered when using their chemicals, thereby establishing a relationship with them which was to continue throughout his career.

He spent his summer vacation back at Sun River, where he photographed work and activities on one of the remaining big horse and cattle ranches (see illustration 2). The pictures sold well to the ranch's owners and employees and were also used in a local stockman's publication. At his father's suggestion – he had now come round to his son's obsession – Clarence started work on converting a vacant room in the store into a photographic laboratory to use during his vacations.

But it was still a hobby, not yet a future. Clarence enrolled at the University of Michigan to take a course in finance. He had little enthusiasm for the subject, but a friend of his father's had promised him a job in his bank at Billings, Montana, after his graduation. Of more interest to him was the fact that his Port Huron High School chemistry teacher had arranged for him to be able to continue his research into photographic chemistry there.

As always, Clarence made use of every spare moment. He enrolled in an art course and found a part-time job for three hours a day in the main portrait studio of Daines and Nichols. He also worked as a staff photographer on the *Michigan Daily*, a paper published by the University Literary Department. He bought a 3¼″ × 4¼″ Graflex press camera to use on his commissions, which included portrait sittings and sporting events. At the latter Bull revealed the quickness of his eye, capturing the blur of a baseball as it was caught by a glove. The paper was soon putting him on assignment to meet any celebrities arriving at Ann Arbor by train. His earliest scoop for them was a photograph of Admiral Robert T. Perry, the discoverer of the North Pole arriving with William Jennings Bryan, Secretary of State and at one time the most celebrated criminal lawyer in America; Clarence always kept the newspaper cutting of this picture attached to an appreciative letter he had received from Admiral Perry. It was at this time, and while working for Daines and Nichols, that he had the opportunity to shoot his first celebrity portrait. Bryan sat for him, and liked the result enough to autograph a copy for Clarence (see illustration 3).

It was 1915. There was a war on in Europe and America had gone movie mad. At this time Bull developed an increasing interest in moving picture work. He had learned to operate an Ernamann 35 mm motion picture camera at Daines and Nichols and had made a documentary film of life on campus for the university. When he was at a football match and a news cameraman became ill, he took over his camera and filmed the game for him. Despite a minor embarrassment during the match when, in his enthusiasm, he strayed onto the pitch, the results were successful and the newsreel company paid him $ 50. Ever practical, he later wrote, "That check was another plus towards my decision to become a motion picture cameraman" (*Unpublished Notes*).

Even before finishing his studies he took his first

3 William Jennings Bryan, 1915. An early professional portrait taken at the studio of Daines and Nichols, Michigan

4 Viola Dana for *Breakers Ahead*, 1918. Clarence Bull's first set photograph

major steps towards his final career. He returned home to set up a photographic business in his hardware store laboratory, by then completed and fully equipped to his own ingenious specifications. There was no gas or electricity so he devised a system for drying prints using a kerosene camp stove. Prints were washed in eight minutes by a system based on an elevated water tank which had to be pumped full each day. Soon he had set up a lucrative printing business, taking local orders through his father's store and receiving more distant ones from drug stores and other sources on the 8 a.m. railway mail which he sent back on the 2 p.m. return train from Great Falls.

It was through one of his customers that Clarence was given his first introduction to the motion picture business. He developed and printed a film for Mrs Frank Lloyd, the wife of the director. By 1917, Lloyd had already directed and written over forty films in his first two years as a director. Born in Glasgow, the son of a musical comedy actor, he appeared on the British stage as an actor at the age of 15. He moved to Canada in 1910, and then to America three years later, first acting in films before becoming a director in 1914. Mrs Lloyd was delighted with the results and, hearing of his ambitions, wrote to recommend Clarence to her husband, then working on a picture at Fort Lee, New Jersey. Frank Lloyd duly replied, offering him a job on his film crew.

Clarence's father was still sceptical, but his mother was on his side, and so he wound up his photographic

business and set off for Fort Lee via Port Huron, where a telegram awaited him saying that they were moving the operation to Hollywood but the offer was still good. Undiscouraged and equipped with his three cameras, an Ingenta, a Voigtländer and a Graflex, he set off for Hollywood. But there, at the Fox Film Company Studios, another message had been left for him: Lloyd had decided to finish the film in Fort Lee after all. This was a setback indeed, and Bull retired to his room at the YMCA to think things over. The next day, armed with a list of Hollywood addresses, he set out to look for a job.

Hollywood

The Mack Sennett Studio was closed but at Metro (formed in 1915) the studio manager Clark Thomas was also from Michigan and was impressed enough with Clarence to give him a trial as assistant cameraman on a new film directed by the Liverpool-born British director Charles Brabin (1882–1957) who later married the first screen vamp, Theda Bara. The film, *Breakers Ahead* (1918) starred Mabel van Buren, Russell Simpson and Metro's leading female star Viola Dana (see illustration 4). On this first film Bull formed friendships that would last through his life. One friendship was with the cameraman John Arnold, the inventor and film pioneer (born 1889) who was Director of Photography on such silent classics as *Show People*

5 Pictorial study for Maurice Tourneur's film *Treasure Island*, 1919

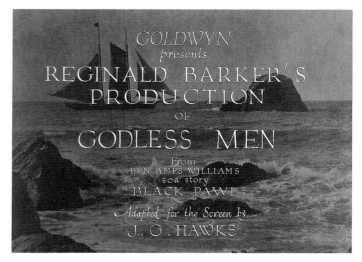

6 Title background for *Godless Men*, 1920

(1928). Arnold was recognized as an outstanding cinematographer and became head of the MGM Camera Department from 1931, a post he held until 1956. In 1919 Bull also worked with the French director Maurice Tourneur on *Treasure Island*. Tourneur was one of the early directors whose films were noted for their painterly compositions and exquisite lighting. His compositional framing and use of lighting must have influenced the impressionable Bull (see illustration 5). As assistant cameraman on *Breakers Ahead*, Bull was delegated the job of filming the titles and, on location in San Francisco, the title background (see illustration 6). *Breakers Ahead* was made entirely with natural light, sunlight with diffusion screens, mirrors and reflectors. When Arnold was injured in a motor cycle accident, Bull had the opportunity to film the final scene. In this, a sea captain was to sit looking at a lifebelt on the wall thinking of his family; Bull suggested that he should make a double exposure in the camera so that a moving picture of the family would appear within the lifebelt. This was a successful early example of photomontage, a technique which Bull was to repeat many times in his work.

Bull made good use of his time at Metro by using production breaks as an opportunity to take informal portraits of the Metro stars such as Mabel Normand, Alla Nazimova, Helene Chadwick, Olive Thomas, and Irene Rich. He also covered each scene with the still camera, and these photographs proved useful for publicity purposes. In the spring of 1918, after only six months at Metro, the studio closed down for re-organization and Clarence was without a job. Six years later, ironically, he returned to work for Metro, then amalga-

mated with Goldwyn and Louis B. Mayer's production company.

Before his next studio contract Clarence found a job in the Imperial Valley, Mexico, with a photographer based in El Centro. He did not stay long however, finding the 100 degree plus heat, not to mention the bugs, uncomfortable. On his return he went to see John Nicklauss, head of photography at Triangle Pictures. Triangle was set up in 1915 to combine the talents of three great directors, D. W. Griffith, Mack Sennett and Thomas H. Ince. The new studios had been built by Ince who had established his name by producing quality Westerns with authentic cowboys and Indians, but by 1918 only Ince was still actively producing films for the failing company. Bull was offered a job as assistant cameraman there and was particularly at home photographing these wild Western

7 Triangle Cowboys, 1918

14

8 Triangle Cowboys, 1918

9 Triangle Cowboys, 1918

scenarios of cowboys performing rope tricks, bucking broncos and other stunts (see illustrations 7, 8 and 9). The Triangle studios were located at Culver City, a suburb of Los Angeles, seven miles south of Hollywood, in a new purpose-built lot fronting onto Washington Boulevard. It was built with an imposing Corinthian-colonnaded frontage that differentiated Triangle from all other Hollywood studios. But by the end of 1918, six months later, Triangle was taken over by Samuel Goldwyn Pictures to become Goldwyn Studios (see illustration 10) but Bull continued to work for Goldwyn at Culver City where he was to stay until his retirement in 1961. He still worked as assistant cameraman at the new company but, more significantly for his true vocation, the perceptive and publicity-conscious Goldwyn, who had been impressed by Bull's photographs for Triangle, asked him to concen-

trate on taking stills and portraits for publicity and put him in charge of this department. "They needed a good portrait photographer", Bull later wrote, "so I guess you could say that the photo department came into being. I was in the right place at the right time" (*Unpublished Notes*). It gave him the opportunity to photograph some of the most celebrated popular writers of the day who came to Hollywood as part of Goldwyn's desire to give the public 'Great Films by Great Authors' (see illustration 11).

The development of Bull's career from cameraman to portrait photographer was a path followed by many others. The careers of other Hollywood photographers such as Ernest Bachrach, Robert Coburn and Eugene Richee followed similar patterns. Richee, later head of the portrait gallery at Paramount studio, had been Bull's assistant at Goldwyn. (In 1941 when Richee had

10 Goldwyn Studios on Washington Boulevard, 1919

11 Samuel Goldwyn with Rex Beach, an unidentified person, Mary Rinehart and Abe Lehr, 1919

been ousted from his post at Paramount, Clarence was able to help out his old friend by offering him work shooting stills at MGM.)

Bull wrote: "Sam believed in publicity photographs by the thousand. From Sam Goldwyn on down, the emphasis was on getting still photographs of his people and his films in the newspapers and the magazines" (*Unpublished Notes*). This aspect of the film business had grown in strength and importance ever since the introduction of the first film magazines catering to the general film public. Their success was immediate, their growth phenomenal. Starting with a few titles in the early 1910s, they had proliferated to more than 60 by the time Bull joined Goldwyn. Not only were there American film publications, but all major magazines had special sections devoted to movies. Europe had its own. In England, from 1919 onwards, periodicals such as *The Tatler*, *The Sketch*, *Illustrated London News* and *The Graphic*, would regularly devote one or more full pages per issue to films. Exhausted from the war, the public's hunger for anything from the American film world was enormous. The concept of the individual film star was already established by the time Clarence first arrived in Hollywood and alongside this had come a new concept in promotion. *Motion Picture Magazine* was first, in 1911, and was followed by *Photoplay*, *Movie Star Parade*, and *Movie Weekly*. Two of the more de luxe titles, *Screenland* and *Shadowland* featured superb tinted rotogravure plates. Photographs of stars, as well as being sent to fans who requested them, were distributed for reproduction free of charge in return for use with a caption crediting the film company and publicizing the film. Bull's stills on Goldwyn films such as *Bitterness of Sweets* (UK title *Look Your Best*, 1923) and *The Grim Comedian* (1923), and his portrait studies of Goldwyn stars such as Helene Chadwick, Lon Chaney, Blanche Sweet, Dagmar Godowsky and Colleen Moore ensured his job and the expansion of his responsibility. Special pictorial features on stars were always popular and one of Bull's first published sets in *Shadowland* featured the idolized opera star Geraldine Farrar with her husband Lou Tellegen posing affectionately in the garden of their Culver City mansion home (see illustration 12). The result was captioned as a 'Romeo and Juliet tableau' and credited as 'a happy thought of the cameraman'. The photographs were to publicize Farrar's arrival in Hollywood to appear in the Goldwyn film *The World And Its Women* (1919) which was

12 Lou Tellegen and Geraldine Farrar, 1919

directed by Frank Lloyd. Two years after arriving in Hollywood Bull at last worked with the man who had been responsible for his leaving Sun Valley for California in the first place. Bull was his assistant cameraman, as well as stills man on this production which was the first of many films on which they would both work (see illustration 13).

The first day's shooting took place in a large ballroom. Clarence was second cameraman, recording the entrance of Tellegen and Farrar. At a crucial moment, Bull's inexpertly taped-up camera fell apart, crashing heavily onto the train of the passing Farrar's dress. Joe

13 Pauline Frederick, with film director Frank Lloyd and assistant cameraman Clarence Bull, 1919

Cohen, production manager, rushed over to demand an explanation. Clarence explained that the tape had melted from the heat of the camera. "So's your job!" Cohen told him. Next day, upon Tellegen's and Lloyd's intercession, Cohen relented, and Bull was reinstated and assigned to set up a camera repair shop.

The next film Bull worked on at Culver City was *The Slim Princess*, directed by Victor Schertzinger, and starring the comedienne Mabel Normand. Bull's portraits of Normand for the film, and his studies of the actress Mae Busch, photographed in her home, are highly accomplished pictorial studies ranking with the best in society studio portraiture of the time. Bull's device of posing Normand in semi-profile against a circular brass tray (see plate 3), or Busch below a batik screen flanked by two urns (see plate 5), are examples of Bull's eye for composition. He avidly studied the work of the major photographers featured in Alfred Stieglitz's *Camerawork*, and was familiar with the best contemporary portraiture published in the leading magazines of the day, such as *Vogue* and *Vanity Fair*, with photographers such as DeMeyer and Steichen (Bull's portrait of Jeanne Eagels in particular adopts the lighting for which DeMeyer made his name). In his unpublished notes, Bull pays tribute to the European photographers who came to Hollywood as cinematographers, such as the British portraitist Charles Rosher, Rene Gissard from France, and Karl Freund from Germany. Seeing their work or working with them helped Bull to assimilate the lessons of their achievements. Perhaps the greatest influence on Bull in the early 1920s was his friendship with Karl Struss, who arrived in Hollywood from New York in 1919 and had worked as an assistant cameraman and special stills photographer on several early Cecil B. DeMille productions before graduating to become one of Hollywood's most distinguished directors of photography through his work on films such as *Ben Hur* (1925). Clarence, who was in Hollywood during the absorption of the Goldwyn company (which had begun the film) into Metro-Goldwyn-Mayer, shot production stills and portraits before and after the production had been to Rome. Struss had studied photography under Clarence H. White and been a member of Stieglitz's Photo-Secession group between 1912 and 1917. Struss, like Bull, was an inventor and camera enthusiast, and patented the special Struss soft focus lens. Bull records an incident which occurred when working on location on a Marion Davies film when a sandstorm blasted his camera lens and produced a soft focus effect, which enchanted Miss Davies, and which he subsequently used on many other occasions. His pictorial soft focus studies of Lillian Gish for *The Wind* (see plate 31), or the Chinese store front *Mr. Wu* (see plate 4) may have been achieved this way, or by using the similar Struss lens.

More effective and certainly more innovative are those portraits created by the lighting style of which he became a master. In his study of Hobart Bosworth (as Shane Keogh in *The Man Alone*, see plate 6) seated by a fireside in a glow created by a concealed arc-light, additional fill-in side lighting illuminates the bric-à-brac filled room, redolent of a life lived at sea; in addition, the posing of the faithful mastiff, creates an atmospheric and spellbinding tableau, reminiscent of a scene painted by Edwin Landseer. It serves as an example of Bull's own story-telling gifts since this photograph had to stand on its own independent of the movie. It also illustrates the unique power of the camera in the right hands to achieve through lighting and technical skill a black-and-white image possessing the richness and emotional power equal to that of a painting without in any way imitating one.

Hobart, in a letter to Bull (23 September 1922), compliments him on his work, "from the extensive coverage of my roles in the pictures since 1908 these (studies) are immeasurably the most beautiful... I don't know which I like the best, the one at the window is superbly lighted and another in which Teddy [the Sennett canine cast as the mastiff] cranes his head on the chair's arm, the pathetic age and weariness, the waiting of the old dog and the old master for the inevitable, is marvellously expressed even to a sort of resemblance, such as one finds in an old couple who have grown alike through association... I can't tell you how proud I am to have them" (*Unpublished Notes*).

The study is sentimental but appropriate to the subject and technically superb. (Twenty years later Bull's study of another faithful dog and his master, Lassie and Roddy McDowall, would win him one of the few Academy Awards given for stills photography.)

The American release of the German film *The Cabinet of Dr Caligari* had a major if temporary effect on still and motion picture photography. The expressionistic sets and cubist backgrounds were adopted and recreated by Bull for a series of studies of Goldwyn stars, including Molly Malone (see plate 9) and Sylvia

Breamer, both of which were published in the December 1921 issue of *Vanity Fair* (Bull's only credited work in this prestigious periodical in the 1920s) and were captioned: "Cubist Photography ... some recent attempts to reduce human beings to geometric patterns." They were published there and in several other periodicals as examples of the "advanced art of Hollywood portraiture". Startling at the time, they are now more of an historical footnote but show that innovation, when it could bring the studio attention, was allowed. Later, at MGM, Bull was under pressure to produce straightforward, evenly-lit pictures which could be easily reproduced on the inferior paper stock of less prestigious but mass-circulated newspapers. At this early stage any and every notice of Bull's and the studio's work was gratefully noted by the publicity department. Writing in the *Megaphone*, the Goldwyn studio's house bulletin (2 March 1920), the paper's editor, J.S. Wodehouse, comments, "In the selection of art pictures for re-production in *Shadowland*, which is the ultra in modern printing and photo play discussion, it is gratifying to note that among art selections from such portrait studios as Alfred Cheyney Johnson, James Abbé, Woodbury, Mishkin and other noted photographers there appears a photograph taken in our own studio gallery by Clarence S. Bull". The other photographers were all established on the East Coast, and here was a photographer based in a California film studio who was being treated as an equal by an East Coast magazine.

Until the early 1920s and the establishment of their own photographic galleries on their lots, studios regularly employed commercial Los Angeles-based studio photographers such as Witzel, Nelson Evans and Edwin Bower Hesser to shoot portraits of their stars. Witzel was regularly employed by the Fox studio, where he took portraits of their stars, such as Theda Bara for her roles as Cleopatra, as Salomé, and her other vampirish creations, as well as cowboy favourites Tom Mix and Buck Jones. These Witzel portraits of Bara are virtually the only records remaining of this early star since only one or two of her films have survived.

These photographers and the many other self-employed freelance photographers working in Los Angeles – Melbourne Spurr, Henry Waxman, Russell Ball, Lansing Brown – all did commissioned work. Their livelihood, though enhanced by their film work, was not exclusively dependent on nor controlled by the studios. As the demand for ever more photographs grew it became logical for the film companies to have photographers in their exclusive employment. By the early twenties all the major companies had established photographic departments, including portrait galleries, on their lots. This decision was not only economic, since they now had complete control over the all-important images of their employees, the men and women who were presented as idealized beings, set apart by special qualities of talent, beauty and remoteness to provide objects for universal fantasy; remote, yet real; untouchable, but recognizable. Nowhere was this policy more enforced than at MGM.

In 1922 Sam Goldwyn left the studio he had founded but it continued on under new management. An organization chart of April 1923 showing Bull as head of the stills department, draws attention to the large bank of talent which Goldwyn had assembled and which for the large part would, like Bull, be inherited by the new company. Most important of all for the future company was their acquisition of Cedric Gibbons, the art director who had come from New York and was to continue to be a close friend and influence on Bull's work throughout their careers at MGM (see plate 93).

The new studio was created in 1924, the result of three existing but small companies, Metro, Goldwyn and Louis B. Mayer Productions, merging to become the latest and largest of the Hollywood studios. From the beginning Metro-Goldwyn-Mayer was famed (thanks to its own shrewd publicity) for having a greater number of stars under contract than any of its rivals. To Louis B. Mayer, the studio chief, everything else was secondary in importance to the recruitment, development and promotion of these vital company assets. Mayer saw the studio as a family unit with himself at the top in a strong paternalistic role. He applied his keen interest in race horses to the caring, grooming, feeding and training of his 'stable' of two-legged stars. In this 'hothouse' atmosphere stars were encouraged, and above all, controlled, so that they should be presented to, and be perceived by the public in the way that Mayer wanted. The vital job of photographer in such a company was enormously prestigious and demanding.

The man in charge of MGM's publicity department was Howard Strickling. Strickling had been brought over from the French Riviera, where he had been in

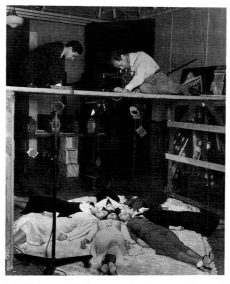

14 Clarence S. Bull and his crew, 1926: Milton Browne, Frank Bjering, Fred Morgan, Homer van Pelt, Merritts Stibold, James Mannett, and Bert Longworth

15 Clarence Bull at work photographing chorus girls for *Broadway Melody of 1936*. Photograph by Tom Evans, 16 April 1935

charge of publicity for the films made there by the mercurial Metro director Rex Ingram. With Metro now part of the new and greater company, and with Ingram making only one film a year, Strickling also found himself in charge of public relations on other overseas productions initiated by any of the three companies, including the runaway biblical epic *Ben Hur*, currently in Rome, beset by production problems that were creating a bad image for the studio, the film's stars and Americans abroad. (One immediate result was an end to American overseas productions for several decades.) Strickling's expert handling of the Italian press over the difficulties erupting between the Americans and the Italians – reports of drowned Italian extras, unpaid wages and orgiastic high jinks – had come to the notice of the new company heads. He was brought to Culver City to become one of the most powerful publicity directors in Hollywood. His taste, tact and discretion were legendary in a town beset by rumours and scandals as explosive as the stars involved in them. By the end of his first decade his department employed over 100 people.

The photography department, with Clarence Bull in charge, was part of Strickling's domain, and now as never before played an increasingly vital role in carrying out the studio's policies.

Stars were an improbability made to seem a possibility. They had to seem 'real'. In an interview Bull gave to *Everyday Photography* (April 1941) he explained his intention: "I always had to make a person look like himself or herself, not like something the person is not." This 'self', once found, was of course held up before the admiring throng as if it were nothing less than the Hope diamond in the flesh. The presentation, the setting of this self, was called 'glamour'. Like diamonds, the image was flawless. Like diamonds, they were priceless. Like diamonds, they were coveted and worshipped. Unlike diamonds, objects only the rich could afford, the stars belonged to everyone. Like the song went, 'The best things in life, are free'.

New recruits to a studio were automatically sent to the gallery as a first step in assessing their ability, while the portraits of established players were an essential part of their presentation to the public who had elevated them to the ranks of the stars. Only, MGM stars had to look bigger, better, brighter, costlier, and more prestigious than any other star at any other studio. That was the MGM style.

A 1926 photograph (see illustration 14) shows Clarence Bull with his crew of nine stills photographers, including Milton Browne, Frank Bjering, Fred Morgan, Homer van Pelt, Merritts Stibold, James Mannett, Bert Longworth, but missing Art Marion who was out on location. It shows the size to which the department had grown and the manpower required to produce the volume of stills for the studio's stars and productions. Bull was in charge of the organization of the stills department. He ensured its smooth running and

16 Chorus girls of *Broadway Melody of 1936* photographed by Clarence Bull, 16 April 1935

illustration 18), George Bernard Shaw (see illustration 19) and Madame Chiang Kai-shek on their tours of the studio. Such was his reputation for excellence.

Most of the production stills work was done by Bull's crew. James Mannett was one of the most talented. He worked on *Trail of '98* and notably on Hedy Lamarr's *Lady of the Tropics*. William Grimes took stills on Gilbert and Garbo's *Love* and some of her subsequent films. Milton Browne was principal stills photographer on Lillian Gish's films and on many of Garbo's talkies such as *Anna Christie, Susan Lennox, Painted Veil,* and *Ninotchka.* Fred Morgan worked on Marion Davies films, Wallace Chewning on Lon Chaney films such as *London after Midnight.* Homer van Pelt was apparently most at home photographing outdoor stories and animal stars, such as Flash in *Dog of War* and trained police dogs as a sideline. Bert Longworth worked on Garbo's first films but his stay at MGM was short and he left to make a major name for himself at Warner Bros. where he was responsible for the spectacular stills from the Busby Berkeley musicals. The surprising omission from the group photograph was Ruth Harriet Louise who had been recruited to MGM in 1925 and

allocated work to each of the individual photographers according to their particular talents.

Bull later itemized 31 different types of use still photographs had in the making of motion pictures, and although many of these would be unseen by the public, they were nevertheless important to the industry. Bull at some time or other worked in most of these categories but as head of stills his principal work was as chief portrait and glamour photographer, working in his own special gallery. This was the most highly regarded and important role for a stills man. On rare occasions he would also take photographs on the set for important and prestigious productions such as for *Broadway Melody of 1936* (see illustrations 15 and 16). He took pictures for 'poster art': photographs which would be adapted and realized in colour with added backgrounds by a poster artist, such as his study of Johnny Weissmuller on a swing (the swing would have been exchanged for a jungle setting) for *Tarzan and His Mate.* One large part of Bull's work was to photograph stars at home, such as Adolphe Menjou playing his piano (plate 74) or Jean Harlow in the swimming pool of her new house in Beverley Glen Drive (plate 97). Other healthy outdoor subjects included Joan Crawford sunbathing at home or signing official photographs taken by Bull for her legion of fans (plate 96). His continuing interest in darkroom experiments could be seen in his use of photomontage when he recreated the excitement of the premiere of MGM's first 'all star' movie, *Grand Hotel* (1932) (see illustration 17).

Another part of his job was to do special studio sittings of visiting dignitaries such as Albert Einstein (see

17 Montage of premiere of *Grand Hotel* at Graumann's Chinese Theatre, 1932

18 Louis B. Mayer and Albert Einstein on the set of the German language version of *The Big House*, 3 February 1931

19 George Bernard Shaw, Marion Davies, Louis B. Mayer, and Clark Gable during a dinner at San Simeon, 27 March 1933

had become John Gilbert's favourite personal portrait photographer, and through him, Garbo's as well. Louise quit MGM in the middle of 1929 to marry director Leigh Jason.

The stills department was housed in three buildings and included developing and printing, retouching and reception areas and offices as well as two portrait galleries. Bull was in charge of one and the second one was used by a succession of portrait photographers. In a studio of such size and with as many stars to constantly promote as MGM boasted, two active and separate portrait galleries were a necessity. At one point in the mid-thirties there were four portrait photographers all working at the studio. Louise was replaced by George Hurrell, who had been expressly recommended by Norma Shearer, wife of production director Irving Thalberg. As explosive as he was brilliant Hurrell stayed only three years. His place was taken by Ted Allan who had joined the studio in 1933 and quickly made a name for himself with his dramatic and unusual production stills and character portraits on films like *Merry Widow* and *A Tale of Two Cities*. After he left, there was Laszlo Willinger from 1937 to 1941. Bull himself gave up most of his day-to-day work in the mid 1940s when his former assistant Virgil Apger, who had moved from assisting Bull in the gallery to covering the Jean Harlow and MacDonald-Eddy films, now took over the No. 1 portrait gallery and remained in charge until 1967.

By the end of the 1920s Bull's work was fairly well known within the film industry and in the specialist press for its workmanlike skill and technical craftsmanship but his elevation to a photographer of the first rank began only with his collaboration with Greta Garbo. As he modestly noted, "The afternoon Garbo told me I was to be the only lensman to make her portraits, even I began to think I was a fair photographer" (*Unpublished Notes*).

Greta Garbo

Bull's first significant session with Garbo was when he came to shoot the portraits for her last silent film *The Kiss* in 1929. "I recall that first morning the great Garbo walked into my portrait gallery looking like a frightened schoolgirl" (*Unpublished Notes*). Garbo, a creature of extreme habit, suddenly found herself confronted with a new photographer having been photographed for the past three years by Ruth Harriet Louise. Most film stars considered their gallery sessions the most uncomfortable and exposing part of their work. Garbo was no different, and was unique in Hollywood in that she only ever posed in character for her role in whatever film she was making, and this may account for her reaction to their first session as Bull recalled it. Though, as he points out, "What she didn't know was that I was just as scared. For three hours I photographed her in every pose and emotion that beautiful face could mirror. At the end of the sitting, which had been without a single break, she said 'I'll do better next time Mr Bull. I was quite nervous.' I patted her hand and replied, 'So will I'" (*Unpublished Notes*).

By 1929 Garbo was one of the major stars of MGM. It was the year of the crash on the New York Stock Exchange and a time of uncertainty. Most of the studios had converted to sound but MGM was apprehensive about their Swedish star, wondering whether or not she would make a smooth transition to talking pictures. Their top male star John Gilbert had made a disastrous sound debut and they postponed Garbo's talking debut until the last moment. It was important that Bull's portraits promoting the silent film she was making should be sensational.

Garbo's rise to fame had been meteoric. In purely financial terms, she had managed to have her salary raised from $600 a week before the opening of *Flesh and the Devil* to $6,000 a week shortly afterwards. This reflected her box office appeal to both male and female movie-goers. To men she was fascinating, mysterious and desirable. To women, she appealed through her beauty and intelligence, her strength and self-reliance; an inspiration of how their romantic lives might be. Part of her mystique was created by her jealously-guarded private life. The creation of her legend was one of the more spectacular achievements of the MGM publicity machine but it needed the undeniable qualities of her real talents and her shy personality to fuel it. Bull, despite his close proximity to her, was in as much awe of her as the rest of America or indeed the world.

The Swedish born Garbo had arrived in Culver City in the summer of 1925 and was at work by November on her first film *The Torrent*, in which she played a fiery Spanish dancer, which was an immediate popular and critical success. The publicity department was at first unsure of how to promote this 'mysterious stranger' (who spoke little English) and planned a series of rather ill-judged publicity photographs. Don Gillum photographed her training with the UCLA athletes in a jersey and running shorts, flexing her muscles. In another session, she was posed by the sea in a bathing costume holding an umbrella like a Mack Sennett beauty. She was also posed cuddling lion cubs from the nearby Selig Zoo, home of MGM's Leo the Lion. These early pictures would continue to haunt her and prompted Garbo to insist on a revised contract which stated that she would only pose directly in connection with her films. After *The Torrent* (1926), she was again cast

20 Greta Garbo. Costume study for *The Temptress*, 1926

as a Latin vamp in *The Temptress* (1926), and was then memorably paired with John Gilbert in the sensational *Flesh and the Devil* (1927). The off-screen romance with Gilbert, who was at that time the cinema's great lover, a role he had inherited after the death of Valentino, added an extra dimension to the film's sensual love scenes. Gilbert used Ruth Harriet Louise as his personal trusted photographer and recommended her to Garbo. The collaboration worked well until Louise left MGM in 1929. It is not clear on how many occasions Bull had photographed Garbo before he became her official gallery photographer. A costume study of her in *The Temptress*, in one of the twenty outfits worn in the film, survives and may be his earliest picture of her (see illustration 20). In *Faces of Hollywood* Bull records that he took some set portraits on *Flesh and the Devil*, though the best-known stills for this film are the portraits taken by Louise and the publicity and advertising shots by Bert Longworth. Bull's outdoor soft focus pictorial studies of Garbo alone under a tree and posed with Gilbert on the set of *Love* (1927) do survive. Since so many stills were not credited in publications, the question of authorship occasionally remains problematic. One of Bull's many useful innovations was to devise and patent a negative numbering procedure. He set up a system whereby the name of the photographer, the date of the photograph, and the department for which it was taken would be recorded on the side of each 10″ × 8″ negative. These details are invaluable for the film historian. Portraits for *The Kiss* were taken on

21 Greta Garbo for *The Kiss*, 1929

22 Poster for *The Kiss*, 1929

27 August 1929. This is the first major Garbo sitting Bull records. From *The Kiss* until *Two Faced Woman* in 1941, Bull was to take all Garbo's portraits with the exception of one film in 1930, *Romance*. George Hurrell, who came to MGM in that year, took these portraits. Writing in 1972, Joan Crawford noted: "Clarence Bull was a very quiet, serious man. He might joke with you before you started the sitting, but once you were in there, he was the most dedicated man imaginable" (*The Image Makers*). Hurrell's approach on the other hand was quite different. Talking constantly, rushing around, Garbo did not find him personally compatible and the experience was not to be repeated. A 1941 news cutting about Garbo, then at work on her last film, by John Chapman for the New York *Sunday News*, relates how an anonymous photographer was assigned to photograph Garbo: "He was a twittery artistic type. He started hopping around and crawling on the studio floor looking for 'angles'. After two shots, Garbo ran out of the studio. 'There's a crazy man in there', she said." George Hurrell himself admitted that it had soon been obvious that he and Garbo were not compatible although the results of their one session produced enough good portraits for the publicity department to promote her new film, and show a surprisingly corporeal Garbo.

Bull's portraits for *The Kiss* are suffused with an elegaic softness and allure. Garbo's outstanding facial characteristics were her eyes with their unusually long lashes. Bull realized the importance of Garbo's eyes to her appeal and for one pose concentrated his lighting to portray only a close-up of her face floating on a darkened background. Garbo's face is further framed above her brow by the curved line of her beret. Her face appears softly modelled in a rapt and engaging expression which communicates directly with the viewer. Compared with most of Louise's studies, which show her eyes averted, Bull's more purposefully frontal approach both in this study and in another where she holds her hands behind her head creates an effect which is equally mesmeric and haunting. The result preserves the 'inner mood' he sought to capture. The darkness of the setting from which Garbo emerges adds to the bewitching spell the pictures create. The potency of the beret photograph was such that it came to be used for the film poster (see illustrations 21 and 22).

For her first talkie, *Anna Christie* (1930), Bull did what the film camera at this stage could not do – he created dramatic close-ups of Garbo illuminated by the glow of a kerosene lamp. Garbo's rapt and attentive expression conveys the doubt and uncertainty she faced as the character in the film. The story, based on the play by Eugene O'Neill, cast Garbo as the down-on-her-luck sea captain's daughter whose father becomes reduced to running a barge. The film's locations include the interior of the barge and its waterfront mooring and much of the action takes place at night. The novelty of Garbo talking in a surprisingly deep and husky voice, coupled with the emotional range that this twenty-five-year-old actress brought to several long monologues, ensured her and the film's critical and popular success. Fifty years later it is Garbo in close-up in Bull's portraits that survives the test of time rather than the film with its creaky settings and unrealistic storm-tossed sequences. The action and dialogue scenes were shown mainly in long shot and appear somewhat stage-bound. Bull's close-ups provided the intensity which the film lacked but which the public, already prepared by his photographs, remembered and brought with them when they saw the film.

With each successive film Bull's lighting of Garbo for their studio sessions shows a different approach from that which he adopted for the other stars. It was generally more subtle and sophisticated and showed signs of the extra care that he was inspired to take. The overall darkness and changing highlights he selected for illumination continued to add to the mystery of his subject and sense of other-worldliness that became part of Garbo's appeal. It should be pointed out that from the time Bull started to photograph Garbo the actress had virtually ceased to pose for any generic photographs, a privilege no other star of her generation was able to command. She never posed strictly as herself. His mood and costume studies for *Mata Hari* are rightly celebrated. Cecil Beaton in his book *Glass of Fashion* copies in a line drawing one of these as the essence of the Garbo appeal, her hair starkly pulled back, her hand to her face, and her eyes looking downwards. It is perhaps Bull's most emblematic composition. Garbo was unlike any other star in the film firmament and Bull's photographs serve to reinforce the difference. The best of them convey a remoteness and intelligence of a woman in charge and aware of her attraction though not certain of her destiny.

Bull gave many interviews about his sessions with Garbo which are interesting for his working methods. Garbo would arrive at his studio punctually at 9 a.m., and worked through till a prompt ending at 5 p.m., the same routine which she observed when filming. Bull bemoaned the fact that none of his other subjects could be relied on to be so prompt and businesslike. Many had to be cajoled, or would arrive late, and need, as he termed it, 'relaxers', in the form of a martini or two before they started work. Virgil Apger, Bull's assistant, recorded how Garbo would often walk barefoot around the gallery in a totally noiseless manner so that at times, after a break, they would not be aware of her.

With each sitting Bull discussed his plans in advance. Garbo was to "move freely in the gallery. When the pose was to my liking I quickly adjusted the lights and made the picture. Miss Garbo read my face out of the corner of her eye and when she saw that I liked an expression there was no need to say 'Still'. Or, 'Hold It...' All I did was to light the face and wait. And watch" (*Unpublished Notes*).

Garbo used to arrive at the gallery with her hairdresser and her maid, already made up. She liked to have music playing on the gramophone, popular tunes such as 'Broadway Rhythm' rather than the classical records Bull imagined she would prefer. He worked with his assistant and an electrician on standby for the lights. Each session would produce two to three hundred eight by ten inch negatives and Garbo would insist on going through all the proofs as they laid them out on the floor. She was quick and decisive as to what she approved and generally ninety per cent of the exposures were passed on to the publicity department which in turn would use them all. Such was the rarity and demand for her photographs. And Bull took them all.

Garbo was his "best subject... The easiest of all stars to photograph ... having no bad side and no bad angles." Her rapport with the camera was such that "she seems to feel the emotion for each pose as part of her personality. Garbo was the most cooperative star I ever worked with, always willing to try the unusual; lighting effects and expressions of inner feelings and conflicts. She never seems to tire of posing. I have known her to hold a pose, either in glaring lights or by the dimmest ones, for more than a minute and a half' (*Unpublished Notes*).

This ability enabled him to take several exposures of one set-up. What made this quality so rare is that most people's expressions, even when they are not smiling, tend to freeze and become unnatural (see plates 80, 87, 88 for *Susan Lennox*).

For his study of her as *Queen Christina* Bull made a ten second exposure so that Garbo was illuminated almost solely by the light of the three candles at which she gazed. The soft, subtle light and the length of the exposure combined to create a three-dimensional and spell-binding portrait (see plate 112). For studies such as this, using minimal lighting to achieve extraordinary effects, Bull first experimented alone in his studio with a plaster bust, investigating ways in which different

23 Greta Garbo as "The Sphinx", montage, 1931

light sources could be juxtaposed to create tableaux reminiscent of the paintings of Georges de la Tour and Caravaggio. Bull's obsession with candle power date back to his early days in Hollywood, and is shown in his portrait of the actor Alec B. Francis (see plate 7) which was one of the series he did of male and female stars. At the end of the 1930s he was photographing Nelson Eddy and Jeanette MacDonald, in near darkness, in a half-lit evocative two-shot study, which was almost a silhouette (see plate 148). With Hedy Lamarr, the exotic European recruited from Vienna, Bull's close-up profile and eyelash studies continue his further exploration on this theme, which reaches its apogee with his singular eclipse lighting study of Garbo for *Ninotchka* (see plate 147). Her face and the background are almost totally invisible but the subject is unmistakably Garbo, her features delineated by the light that etches the contour of her face and neck. Such a picture only works with a subject as recognizable as Garbo. This technique enabled Bull to create a photographic *tour de force* predating the strobe-lit effects of the 1950s, with which Gjon Mili recorded the creation of Picasso paintings.

Garbo's succession of costume roles from the mid-thirties onward, in films like *Queen Christina*, *Anna Karenina*, *Camille* and *Conquest*, her wardrobe designed by Adrian, allowed Bull a tremendous opportunity to create visions of luxury and opulence. His *Camille* pictures are the kind of magical studies of which Winter-

halter would have been proud. "Garbo actually works harder when posing for portraits than she does before the motion picture camera... She considers the posing as part of her screen work and feels absolute concentration is necessary to get emotion over to the still camera" (*Unpublished Notes*).

Most of Garbo's roles were intensely serious and it was not until *Ninotchka* that she was finally able to show her gift for comedy. This was an aspect of her character that she regretted not showing more often in her films, though there exist many wonderful earlier studies of her laughing and smiling for Bull's camera. But clearly, making a film in which she could laugh, without regret, affected her. Bull noted how as a change from music on the gramophone she switched to radio comedy programmes.

Garbo's un-American desire for privacy and her refusal to give interviews led to her being dubbed with many nicknames, but the one that stuck was 'The Swedish Sphinx'. Bull could claim credit for this. In 1931 he decided to experiment in the darkroom. Taking a vignette close-up study of Garbo's face he re-exposed it over a photograph of the Cairo Sphinx, having previously airbrushed out its face. Rather timorously he showed the results to Garbo, thinking she might be offended but was instead greeted with howls of laughter, and then as quickly begged his pardon in case she had offended him with her laughter. She approved it (see illustration 23). The studio was thrilled. The picture was distributed throughout the world and became one of the most widely reproduced of her images. In the 1940s, when Salvador Dali went to Hollywood to work on a film, he would create a similar portrait in film and paint of Shirley Temple (!) as the Sphinx.

In the mid-thirties, after ten years as chief portrait photographer, the publicity department was considering promoting Bull out of the gallery into a more senior administrative role which would have put an end to his photography but, as Virgil Apger told historian John Kobal, Garbo insisted that no one else could take her portraits, and as the studio's most prestigious property, even though by this time she was making only one film every 18 months, her wishes were respected.

Throughout the 1930s Bull worked in his studio refining his lighting set-ups and techniques which could be adapted to suit the individual and differing needs of his subjects. Props in his best pictures were used only sparingly such as in his portrait of Herbert Marshall (see plate 123) where the use of shadow and an art deco figure helps transform what would otherwise be a dull subject. Bull was on friendly terms with many of the MGM stars. He spent weekends on Johnny Weissmuller's yacht and went to great pains in his studies of the first 'talkie' Tarzan. His swimming suit study of Weissmuller posed with arms outstretched is instantly reminiscent of George Hoyningen-Huene's elegant *Vogue* fashion photographs which have since become classics. Bull may have been aware of these or the similarity could be coincidental. Certainly Bull's 1932 study of Veree Teasdale taken while walking on the MGM lot anticipates by five years Martin Munkasci's now famous but similar studies of Jean Harlow which were published in one of the first issues of *Life* as examples of an exciting new style of celebrity portraiture.

George Hurrell, and later Laszlo Willinger, who also worked at the studio, had some influence on his style but Bull was never happy deviating too far away from the mainstream style that he himself had developed.

Bull was most proud of his major technical innovations. In the 1950s he was in close contact with Harold M. Egerton about the introduction of strobe lighting for colour photography. In this and the introduction of the spot or boom light for close-ups he was a pioneer. Bull's use of the spotlight came about through photographing Jean Harlow, the 'platinum' blonde. She had been upset by the fact that in many of her photographs either her hair had appeared burnt-out because the bright overhead arc lights had reacted to its extreme lightness, or else the hair would be right but her skin tones all wrong. Soon after she joined MGM in 1932 she came to Bull for advice. Bull first photographed Harlow on the set of *Red Dust* after her day's filming was over. He noticed on an adjoining lot the set for a hospital drama. It was being dismantled but one of the properties was a small surgeon's lamp. He appropriated it to use as a light to beam on her hair. The desired effect was achieved and Bull nicknamed the light 'Harlow's Halo'. "It worked like a charm, adjusting to any angle, or any amount of light. I knew the prints would be perfect. Jean's hair glowed, and afterwards she hugged and kissed me breathless" (*Unpublished Notes*). (See plate 68.)

Clark Gable was another of Bull's favourites. He had first photographed and captured the animal magnetism of Harlow with Gable while they were making the

steamy plantation drama *Red Dust* (1932). Those studies show Bull's particular skill at portraying the sexual chemistry of screen-matched couples – the positioning, the body language and the expressions of people whose primary romance is before and with a camera. Though Harlow and Gable had appeared together in an earlier film this was the first time their magnetism had been exploited with real success. Bull also shot their fifth and last appearance together in a gallery, when they were making *Saratoga* (1937). Though Gable had many other leading ladies, there was always something special about the Gable-Harlow team. These last shots by Bull are particularly poignant because, taken shortly before her sudden and unexpected death, they capture the particular harmony between these two screen lovers who had become friends. Bull relates that Harlow had a premonition of her early death and the photographic session was set up while the film was still in production, rather than, as was usual, after the film was completed. His studies show two beautifully groomed and vibrant actors at the peak of their careers in a highly romantic and elegant juxtaposition.

One of the advantages that a photographer employed full time by a studio had over any outsider who was given a single commission, however artistically renowned that outsider might be, was that the studio's photographer had the opportunity to build up a professional relationship with his subjects, to discover their strengths and weaknesses, their fears, how best to handle them, and how to make a strong point seem, when accentuated, to be the essence of their personality. Some of Bull's subjects, like Jeanette MacDonald (who always preferred to have her portraits taken by Clarence) or Carole Lombard (on a loan-out from Paramount) were easy to work with. His most reluctant sitter, indeed every photographer's most reluctant sitter, was Spencer Tracy. Fortunately Bull was luckier than the others since he had Katharine Hepburn to help him cajole Tracy into the gallery (see plate 164). Some stars, Eleanor Powell for example, enjoyed company while they were being photographed. Some, like Hedy Lamarr preferred to be alone. But, while everybody wanted to photograph the beautiful Lamarr, only to find her one of the more wooden camera subjects around, Clarence overcame this problem by concentrating on filling his lens with her face instead of trying to get her to strike an unusual pose. With her he sought no mystery, it was enough to record that spectacular beauty. With some stars it was a question of timing. Errol Flynn, Spencer Tracy, W.C. Fields and John Barrymore, heavy drinkers all, were best photographed in the mornings. "Better get your pictures before noon, Clarence", Flynn told him when he first came to work at MGM in 1948. When he photographed Joan Crawford, always in advance of the latest fashion and make-up fads and wanting to be photographed in all of them, she insisted one time on wearing too much lipstick, a problem that had to be solved by the retouching.

Bull was known for his sympathetic approach and would, as with his Garbo sittings, often play music to establish a relaxed mood. In this he was much like any of the other photographers. "Gary Cooper and James Stewart would pull faces between shots to relax their facial muscles and avoid a set expression. A bit like a tenor limbering up the larynx before going out on stage to sing. Myrna Loy would do this by closing her eyes. Gable would pace up and down. Then he'll think of something interesting to tell me – that's when I click the shutter" (*Unpublished Notes*). Gable shared Bull's passion for hunting.

In his long years at MGM Bull had many such opportunities to build up a relationship of trust with his subjects. Like every important photographer he had his favourite subjects, and stars who favoured him for their portraits even with new and sometimes more exciting photographers on the lot. With time, he would find himself in the role of father confessor to a new generation of stars to whom he was something of an affectionate legend, 'the man who shot Greta Garbo' – as when sixteen-year-old Elizabeth Taylor cried because her mother wouldn't allow her to go out on dates; or when he locked Vivien Leigh and Laurence Olivier alone together in his gallery after one of her sittings for *Gone With The Wind* to give them some privacy and enable them to settle some misunderstanding between them without anybody else getting in the way. Or when the young Ava Gardner came to his gallery for a pin-up session and confided her worries that Mayer was not going to renew her contract. Bull took her off for cocktails and fatherly advice before they got down to work.

Photographing stars in their homes had its hazards. Swimming pools especially could be treacherous, and he accidentally fell into both Colleen Moore's and Carole Lombard's pools during sessions at their homes.

Then, when he went swimming with Harlow in her pool (see plate 97) after photographing her everywhere in her newly built house, he had to dive to search for the bottom of her costume which she claimed had fallen off in the water. "I never could open my eyes under water ... until that emergency. When I finally came up for air empty-handed, Jean told me she'd found it herself." He might, he said, "have suspected that she was playing a practical joke on me, but there she was, wearing it inside out" (*Unpublished Notes*).

In the 1940s, after Garbo's last film, *Two Faced Woman* (1941), Bull spent less time on studio portraiture and more on administration, studio public relations and supervising a new group of younger photographers. In 1942 he was put in charge of emergency courses training soldiers in the signal and Marine Corps in the use of photography for reconnaissance and other military purposes, at the United States government's request, as part of the Motion Picture Industry's contribution to the war effort.

Bull, with his reputation as Garbo's portraitist, was still much in demand as a photographer of the bright new younger generation of stars of the 1940s such as Ava Gardner, Lana Turner, Esther Williams and Katharine Hepburn. Hepburn's career was relaunched by the success of *The Philadelphia Story* (1940) and continued to grow in magnitude with the series of highly successful films in which she was paired with Spencer Tracy. Bull transformed Judy Garland from an ordinary looking teenager photographed for *Ziegfeld Girl* in 1940 to the highly glamorous actress in the coming-of-age portrait he took of her in 1943 for *Presenting Lily Mars*.

In the 1930s Paramount approached MGM about the possibility of lending out Bull for a series of photographs of their star Marlene Dietrich whom they wished to build up as a second Garbo by photographing her in the same way. "I refused", Bull records in an undated magazine article. Later, some time after she had left Paramount, Dietrich herself made a private appointment: "When she saw my proofs, she threw me that enigmatic smile and said, 'You're better than they say'. I smiled, 'And you're no Garbo.'" Bull concludes the anecdote "She thanked me for that" (*Unpublished Notes*). Bull's skill was not such that he would contrive to make every subject conform to a particular type but rather that he could bring out in each subject an extra dimension of their personality and present it as an aspect of their image. Bull photographed Dietrich again, when she made her only MGM film, *Kismet*, on loan in 1943.

The advent of colour crucially affected portraiture in the 1940s. The latter part of 1939 saw the release of *The Wizard of Oz* and *Gone With The Wind* – two major productions in Technicolor. 1940 would see the release of 18 Technicolor films.

Although throughout the decade the black-and-white film and portrait would continue to be the norm, there would be increasing incentives to experiment with colour. It was thus appropriate that MGM's 20th birthday should be recorded with a colour photograph of its stars for a *Life* exclusive. Several of the major stars were absent. Lana Turner was away on maternity leave, Judy Garland on a concert tour, Charles Laughton touring army camps. Clark Gable, Robert Montgomery, Melvin Douglas and Lew Ayres were in the forces. Herbert Marshall and Robert Walker were ill, while Ann Sothern, Margaret O'Brien and Laraine Day were all absent for different reasons. Nevertheless the picture of Mayer and 64 of the company's leading players was a major coup for studio publicity. *Life* magazine had been started in 1936 and fed eagerly on Hollywood for many of its features, usually using its own staff photographers. On this particular occasion the photographer they sent was equipped with a press camera which was unable to cover adequately the depth of field of the six rows of stars. Bull also photographed (for the studio's own use) the set-up with his large format camera and it was his uncredited picture that was run as a double-page feature in the 26 September issue of *Life*.

Colour prints for exhibition had to be made using the expensive and complicated dye transfer process. The effect this process produced was not entirely true to life, but had an inbuilt drama and vividness that well suited the depiction of the slightly unreal world of the Hollywood star and the great musicals of the time. Lucille Ball's extraordinary bright orange hair could be set off against the carefully chosen green costume (plate 175) for a remarkably striking effect. In his portrait of Cyd Charisse (plate 167), Bull adapts to the incredible possibilities offered by the play of light on coloured and different textured surfaces. The olive skin of Charisse's bare arms is set against the salmon and orange of her dress. A golden cushion lies on a blue satin quilt. Colour was a challenging palette with which to portray the screen's new legends. Bull usually covered each session with two cameras simultaneously using black-and-white film in the second camera, thus giving a double choice of images to distribute to the eager press. The wild, gaudy and livid hues of the 1940s gave way in the 1950s to more subtle and restrained colour renderings made possible by the improved film stock. His portrait of Leslie Caron (see plate 179) illustrates this colouring. This in turn gave way to the greater naturalism of the late 1950s shown in Bull's study of Grace Kelly in her publicity portrait for *High Society* (see plate 182).

Bull had experimented with colour since his first arrival in Hollywood. The earliest colour effects had been produced by hand-tinting as in his portrait of Mabel Ballin as Becky Sharpe in *Vanity Fair* (1923) (plate 10). Many of Bull's other portraits were produced as magazine covers or as art supplements in the form of paintings based on his compositions. The technical possibilities of real colour photography had been possible from the mid-twenties but the expense and the crudeness of the effects it achieved meant that it was not worth pursuing until later. Bull first photographed Garbo in colour for *Camille* but his monochrome studies when printed on cream paper which appear in tones of sepia achieve a far greater aesthetic effect. It is only in the 1940s that Bull mastered the new possibilities. In the late 1950s Bull experimented with different film materials printed on a combination of print stocks to help to solve some of the problems encountered in photographing Van Gogh's paintings for use as reproductions in the Kirk Douglas film, *Lust for Life* (1956). This was one of the prestige productions that Bull worked on in the 1950s. Others included *The Brothers Karamazov* (1958) for which Bull photographed Maria Schell and Claire Bloom. *Cat on a Hot Tin Roof* (1958) was one of the last films for which he took portraits of Elizabeth Taylor, for whom he had a special affection because he had photographed her during her years as a highly ambitious child and teenage actress. Interestingly Bull's career at MGM came almost full circle when one of the last important sittings he took was for the 1959 production of *Ben Hur*, one of MGM's first releases in 1925.

For most of the 1950s Bull acted as a travelling ambassador for the studio. He journeyed to over 20 major American cities at MGM's expense, lecturing on his approach to portraiture and demonstrating how to take photographs in the Hollywood glamour style. The sessions with school groups, photographic societies and other special interest audiences were extremely popular. In 1956 his audience was the biggest ever assembled (over 5,000 delegates) at one of the annual Professional Photographers of America conventions held in Chicago. He repeated this three years later in Los Angeles. The same year he received, what was to him 'his most cherished award', when he was made Honorary Master of Photography of this leading professional body.

Bull, in retirement, saw the style of his photography almost completely disappear and become replaced by the use of a photo-journalistic 'grab-shot' type of picture which aimed to give a truer-to-life record of actors in films. But fortunately, before the end of his life he witnessed a revival in interest in the great years of the Hollywood studios and the star system, with the 1974 exhibition, 'Hollywood Still Photography 1927 to 1941', held in London's Victoria and Albert Museum, which was restaged appropriately close to Hollywood in The Barnsdall Park Municipal Art Gallery in 1975, attracting serious critics of Hollywood portraiture for the first time.

In 1979, in the last few months of his life, Bull was at work producing a limited edition portfolio of his Garbo prints which had been rediscovered by a new discerning type of collector. One of the first auctions ever held of photographs took place in Sotheby's Los Angeles in the early months of 1979. One of the star lots was a Bull portrait of Garbo. Subsequent sales and exhibitions have confirmed the value put on Bull's work and his status as a photographer of importance in the history of photography. The man who shot Garbo today ranks as one of the great portrait photographers of his age.

Plates

1 Helen Ferguson and Lillian Hall in *Going Some* 1920

2 'Deserted' film set 1922

3 Mabel Normand for *The Slim Princess* 1920

4 Set for *Mr. Wu* 1927

5 Mae Busch 1922

6 Hobart Bosworth for *The Man Alone* 1922

7 Alec B. Francis for *The Man Who Saw Tomorrow* 1921

8 Scene for Frank Lloyd's *The Grim Comedian* 1921

9 Molly Malone 1921

10 Mabel Ballin as Becky Sharpe for *Vanity Fair* 1923

11 Shannon Day 1923

12 Bessie Love 1921

13 Antonio Moreno and Colleen Moore for *Look Your Best* 1923

14 Corinne Griffith 1921

15 Helene Chadwick 1921

16 George Walsh 1923

17 Jerusalem set for *Ben Hur* 1924

18 Carmel Myers as the Countess Fedora for *Slaves of Desire* 1923

19 Elinor Glyn 1920

20 Pauline Starke for *Lost and Found on a South Sea Island* 1923

21 Joan Crawford for *Pretty Ladies* 1925

22 Jeanne Eagels for *Man, Woman and Sin* 1927

23 Joan Crawford 1925

24 Wallace Beery 1920s

25 Mae Murray for *The Merry Widow* 1925

26 Tim McCoy and Gwen Lee as George Washington and Betsy Ross 1927

27 Claire Windsor as Betsy Ross in *The Making of the First Flag* 1926

28 Greta Garbo and John Gilbert as Anna Karenina and Vronsky for *Love* 1927

29 Leatrice Joy 1928

30 Greta Garbo as Anna Karenina for *Love* 1927

31 Lillian Gish for *The Wind* 1927

32 Anna May Wong for *Across the Pacific* 1927

33 Tim McCoy 1927

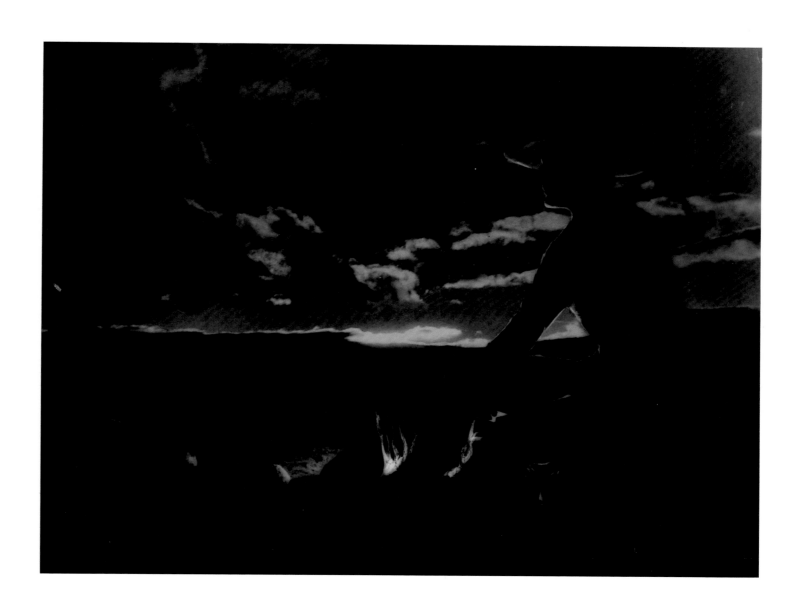

34 Tim McCoy for *Wyoming* 1927

35 Ann Dvorak and Raquel Torres 1929

36 Ralph Forbes 1928

37 Conrad Nagel 1928

38 Greta Garbo for *The Kiss* 1929

39 Greta Garbo for *The Kiss* 1929

40 Greta Garbo as Anna Christie 1929

41 Greta Garbo for *The Kiss* 1927

42 Buster Keaton 1930

43 Edwina Booth as 'The White Goddess' for *Trader Horn* 1930

44 Lupe Velez for *The Squaw Man* 1931

45 Anita Loos 1932

46 Joan Crawford 1930

47 Bessie Love 1930

48 John, Ethel and Lionel Barrymore 1932

49 Virginia Cherrill 1933

50 Helen Twelvetrees 1932

51 San Simeon 1931

52 Marion Davies 1932

53 Marie Dressler 1932

54 Jimmy Durante 1932

55 Diana Wynyard 1933

56 Leslie Howard 1931

57 Paulette Goddard 1932

58 Lillian Bond 1931

59 Carole Lombard 1934

60 Marion Davies 1932

61 Bing Crosby 1933

62 Charles Boyer 1931

63 W. S. Van Dyke 1933

64 Johnny Weissmuller 1933

65 Robert Montgomery 1930

66 Johnny Weissmuller 1934

67 Jean Harlow 1932

68 Jean Harlow and Clark Gable for *Red Dust* 1932

69 Jean Harlow 1930

70 Jean Harlow 1932

71 Norma Shearer and Gilbert Adrian 1932

72 Clark Gable 1931

73 Veree Teasdale, Mrs. Adolphe Menjou 1932

74 Adolphe Menjou 1931

75 Walt Disney 1933

76 Jackie Cooper 1931

77 Gary Cooper 1934

78 Gary Cooper 1934

79 Greta Garbo as Susan Lennox 1931

80 Greta Garbo as Susan Lennox 1931

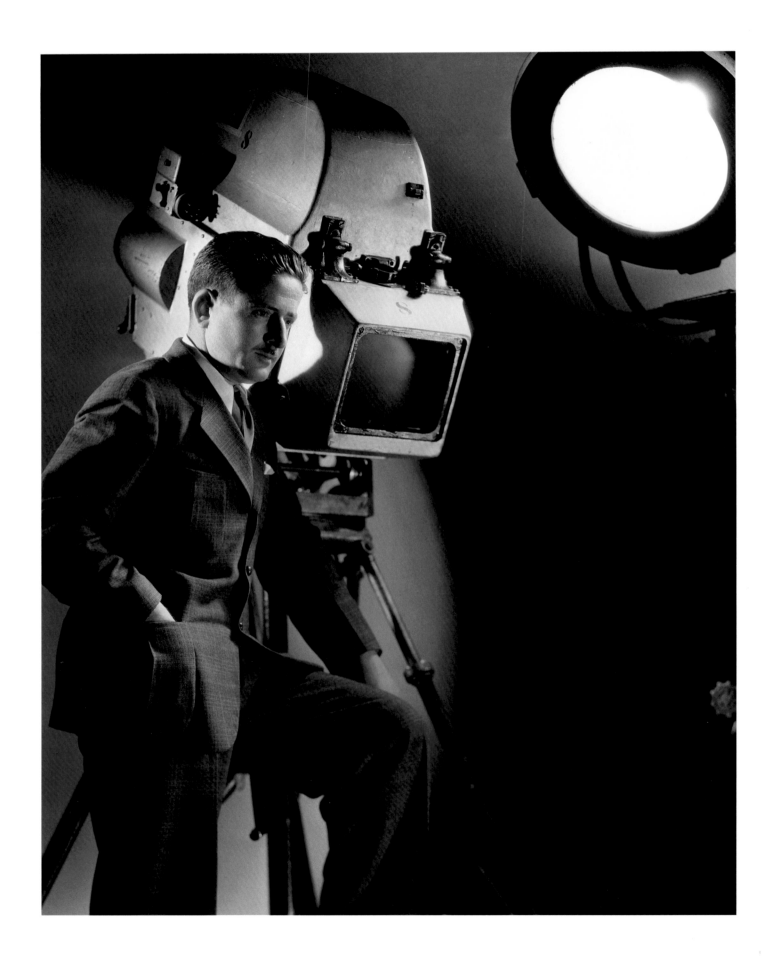

81 William Daniels 1933

82 'Chris' (Garbo's stand-in) 1931

83 Greta Garbo in Mata Hari's dance costume 1931

84 Greta Garbo for *As You Desire Me* 1932

85 Greta Garbo for *Inspiration* 1930

86 Greta Garbo as Mata Hari 1931

87 Greta Garbo as Susan Lennox 1931

88 Greta Garbo as Susan Lennox 1931

89 Greta Garbo for *As You Desire Me* 1932

90 Greta Garbo for *Inspiration* 1930

91 Greta Garbo as Mata Hari 1931

92 Boris Karloff for *The Mask of Fu Manchu* 1932

93 Cedric Gibbons and Dolores del Rio 1931

94 Art-deco revolving entrance for *Grand Hotel* 1932

95 Joan Crawford 1933

96 Joan Crawford 1933

97 Jean Harlow at home 1932

98 Jean Harlow 1934

99 Jean Harlow 1932

100 Madge Evans 1931

101 Mary Carlisle 1933

102 Gloria Swanson 1934

103 Gloria Swanson 1934

104 Tallulah Bankhead 1932

105 Constance Bennett 1934

106 Lewis Stone 1931

107 Otto Kruger 1934

108 Elizabeth Allan 1934

109 Evelyn Laye 1934

110 Greta Garbo for *Painted Veil* 1934

111 Greta Garbo as Queen Christina 1933

112 Greta Garbo as Queen Christina 1933

113 Jeanette MacDonald 1934

114 Loretta Young 1933

115 Miriam Hopkins 1933

116 Maurice Chevalier 1934

117 Elsa Lanchester 1934

118 Charles Laughton 1935

119 Frank Lloyd 1935

120 Charles Laughton as Captain Bligh in *Mutiny on the Bounty* 1935

121 William Powell 1935

122 Ethel Barrymore 1932

123 Herbert Marshall 1934

124 Ray Milland 1930

125 Benita Hume 1934

126 Ronald Colman as Sydney Carton in *A Tale of Two Cities* 1935

127 Freddie Bartholomew as David Copperfield 1935

128 W. C. Fields as Mr Micawber in *David Copperfield* 1934

129 Myrna Loy and William Powell for *After the Thin Man* 1936

130 The Marx Brothers 1935

131 The Marx Brothers for *A Night at the Opera* 1935

132 The Albertina Rasch dancers for *Broadway Melody* during a rehearsal break 1935

133 Eleanor Powell for *Broadway Melody* 1935

134 Deanna Durbin 1936

135 Judy Garland for *Every Sunday* 1936

136 Greta Garbo for *Camille* 1936

137 Greta Garbo for *Camille* 1936

138 Jean Harlow and Clark Gable 1937

139 Jean Harlow and Clark Gable 1937

140 Luise Rainer as O Lan in *The Good Earth* 1936

141 Eleanor Powell for *Honolulu* 1939

142 Greta Garbo for *Conquest* 1937

143 Greta Garbo for *Conquest* 1937

144 Robert Taylor and Hedy Lamarr for *Lady of the Tropics* 1939

145 Hedy Lamarr 1938

146 Hedy Lamarr 1938

147 Greta Garbo for *Ninotchka* 1939

148 Jeanette MacDonald and Nelson Eddy for *Bitter Sweet* 1940

149 Hedy Lamarr 1939

150 Clark Gable and Vivien Leigh for *Gone With The Wind* 1939

151 Clark Gable 1939

152 Clark Gable and Vivien Leigh 1939

153 Katharine Hepburn for *The Philadelphia Story* 1940

154 Eleanor Powell and Fred Astaire for *Broadway Melody* 1940

155 Harry James 1943

156 Katharine Hepburn 1941

157 Cary Grant 1940

158 Judy Garland for *Presenting Lily Mars* 1943

159 Peter Lorre for *They Met in Bombay* 1941

160 Hedy Lamarr 1940

161 Katharine Hepburn for *Without Love* 1944

162 Edmund Gwenn and Pal for *Lassie Come Home* 1943

177 Maria Schell 1958

163 Pal 1940s

164 Spencer Tracy and Katharine Hepburn for *Without Love* 1945

165 Lana Turner and Clark Gable for *Honky Tonk* 1941

166 Greta Garbo for *Two Faced Woman* 1941

167 Cyd Charisse 1947

168 Lana Turner 1943

169 Ava Gardner 1947

170 Robert Mitchum 1946

171 Elizabeth Taylor 1948

172 Marlene Dietrich 1943

173 Ava Gardner 1947

174 Joan Greenwood 1954

175 Lucille Ball 1943

176 Angela Lansbury 1947

178 Louis Jourdan, Leslie Caron and Maurice Chevalier for *Gigi* 1958

179 Leslie Caron 1953

180 Claire Bloom 1958

181 Shirley MacLaine 1959

182 Grace Kelly for *High Society* 1956

183 Grace Kelly 1956

Plate Captions

John Kobal

1 Helen Ferguson (1901–77) with Lillian Hall at the gates of the Goldwyn studios at Culver City. Ferguson acted in films from the age of 13, graduating from extras to featured roles in action dramas; she went to Hollywood when she was signed by Goldwyn in 1919 and retired with the advent of sound to become a press-agent. (*Going Some*, 1920)

2 'Deserted', a pictorial study. A view of a deserted film set on a rare rainy day in southern California on the Goldwyn back-lot, taken in 1922, and first exhibited in a show mounted by the Southern Californian Camera Club at the Southwest Museum in January 1923.

3 Mabel Normand (Muriel Fortescue) (1894–1930). A portrait study for *The Slim Princess* (1920). The daughter of a vaudeville pianist, cheerful Mabel made her film debut in 1911 and quickly became an enormously popular comedienne in countless Sennett shorts and features; she was one of the original legendary Keystone players, working opposite many of the great clowns of the silent era, including Chaplin and Fatty Arbuckle. By 1920, the time of this portrait, Mabel had become one of the highest paid stars in the industry after leaving her lover and mentor Mack Sennett to sign with the newly formed Goldwyn company. The following year she returned to Sennett. Her career was in ruins by 1922, after the tabloid press chose to link her name to two murders.

4 Mood study of deserted set built for Lon Chaney film, *Mr. Wu* (1927).

5 Mae Busch (1897–1946). Australian actress of American silent films including Von Stroheim's classic *Foolish Wives* (1922), but better remembered as the comic harridan who makes life hell for our heroes in a number of Laurel and Hardy shorts of the thirties. Bull took this study which appeared in the January 1923 issue of *Screenland* when she was playing leading lady parts at the Goldwyn studio, usually as a 'vamp' (1922).

6 Hobart Bosworth (1867–1943). Generally regarded as the first important stage star from New York to enter movies in California, he arrived there in 1909. He formed his own company, Bosworth Production, to make films based on the Jack London stories, including *The Sea Wolf* (1913), one of the first feature-length movies made in America, and remained active in films long after his career as leading man was over. This study was taken in 1922 for *The Man Alone*. Beside him, as his 'best friend', is Teddy, the popular Sennett canine. A Great Dane, in movies almost all of his life, Teddy was the first animal ever to be featured in credits. He made his screen debut as a one-year-old in 1915 and quickly leapt ahead to become the best-known animal in movies. His most famous part came opposite Gloria Swanson in *Teddy at the Throttle* (1917). A natural in front of the cameras, Teddy did not know a single trick, and his trainer, Joe Simpkins, would not allow him to be taught any in case it spoiled his uncanny intelligence.

7 Alec B. Francis (1869–1934). A British actor and former barrister, seen here in a character study based on his role in *The Man Who Saw Tomorrow* (1922), he appeared in American movies from 1911 and went on to play major supporting roles such as the King of Hearts in the 1933 version of *Alice in Wonderland*.

8 A scene from *The Grim Comedian* (1921) directed by Bull's friend Frank Lloyd, with sets designed by Cedric Gibbons (see plates 17 and

93), who, along with Clarence, would become one of the bulwarks and mainstays of the MGM studio style.

9 Molly Malone (1895–1952). This picture, published in the December 1921 issue of *Vanity Fair*, shows the stylistic impact the German expressionist film *The Cabinet of Dr Caligari* made on American films and photographers in its mood and set. Malone's best-known roles were in action dramas and in Westerns, many directed by the young John Ford.

10 Mabel Ballin (1885–1958), wife of the famous portrait painter, production designer and film director Hugo Ballin, as Becky Sharpe in *Vanity Fair* (1923). Hugo Ballin was initially hired by Goldwyn to create sets for his films but as director he made a number of elaborate adaptations of literary classics, most of them starring Mabel.

11 Shannon Day. A former 'Follies girl', she came to movies, like so many others from that stage, in the early 1920s. A small, waif-like creature, she appeared in films including the sea-epic *All the Brothers were Valiant* (1923) with Lon Chaney, often as a used and discarded object of men's brutal affection. This pictorial outdoor study conveys the little New York dancer's faun-like appeal.

12 Bessie Love (Juanita Horton) (1898–1987) began her screen career in 1915 as an extra in the classic *Birth of a Nation*, directed by D. W. Griffith, who also changed her name to Bessie Love. She was nominated for an Oscar for her role in the all-singing, all-talking, all-dancing and partially-coloured *Broadway Melody* (1929), her first talkie. After two years of similar and ultimately unpopular films in Hollywood, Bessie continued her career in England, where she settled in 1935, working on stage and screen. One of her last film appearances was in *Ragtime* (1981). This saucy pin-up, more Juanita than Bessie, was taken in 1921.

13 Antonio Moreno (Antonio Garride Monteagudo) (1887–1967) and Colleen Moore (Kathleen Morrison) (1900–1988) in a scene from *Look Your Best* (1923). This film was directed by the author turned director Rupert Hughes who came to Hollywood in 1919 as part of Sam Goldwyn's 'Eminent Films by Eminent Authors' scheme. Colleen Moore had, by this time, become the epitome of the 'flaming youth' of the Roaring Twenties, and the British title, *Look Your Best*, certainly does suggest her box-office appeal.

14 Corinne Griffith (1896–1979). When, towards the end of Corinne's life, her last and much younger husband brought a law-suit claiming that she had deceived him about her age, the still lovely Corinne (who had also become a successful novelist) denied in court that she had once been the 'Orchid Lady' of the screen, one of the most celebrated beauties of silent days in order to keep her age a secret. Bull's portrait of Corinne was taken in 1921, when she was newly married to her first husband Webster Carroll. Corinne's last starring (though not her last) role was in a British-made talkie *Lily Christine* (1932), after which she retired rich and became a writer.

15 Helene Chadwick (1897–1940), blonde leading lady of silent films. She was married to the director William Wellman.

16 George Walsh (1892–1981). Younger brother of actor/director Raoul Walsh, he appeared in *Intolerance* (1916) and was originally cast as *Ben Hur* only to be replaced by rapidly-rising romantic favourite Ramon Novarro when Goldwyn merged with Metro in 1924. This marked the end of George's starring days. Bull took this shot in 1923 when Walsh was announced for the role.

17 A pictorial study of the miniature set of Jerusalem designed by Cedric Gibbons and built in Hollywood for use in *Ben Hur* (1925).

18 Carmel Myers (1899–1980) entered films when D. W. Griffith hired her in return for a favour her rabbi father had done for him when he was making *Intolerance* (1916). Carmel frequently played 'vamps'. In her heyday she co-starred with Valentino, John Barrymore and John Gilbert, and she had a fairly active career on screen and radio well into the 1940s before successfully going into cosmetics, but she was best remembered for her role of Iras, the temptress of Ramon Novarro's *Ben Hur*. This study shows her in costume for one of her typical 'vamp' roles, as the Countess Fedora in *Slaves of Desire* (1923). Carmel's cousin was the photographer Ruth Harriet Louise, who had the other portrait gallery at MGM in the 1920s.

19 Elinor Glyn (1864–1943). In 1906, with the publication of her lurid novel *Three Weeks*, Miss Glyn became as notorious and successful as the 1980s authors Judith Krantz and Jackie Collins. Her popular appeal made her works inevitable candidates for the screen. In 1919, along with Rex Beach, Rupert Hughes, Maurice Maeterlinck and others, she arrived in Hollywood as part of Sam Goldwyn's highly touted 'Eminent Films by Eminent Authors' series. Little came of it. Maeterlinck, author of *The Blue Bird*, laboured

long and before returning to his home in Belgium he gave Goldwyn his script for a film based on the life of a bee. Most of the other authors also went back home, but Miss Glyn remained to cast her spell across the impressionable decade with stories and titles such as *The Great Moment, Love's Blindness, Bed of Roses* and *It*.

20 Pauline Starke (1900–1974). She made her debut in Griffith's *Intolerance*, as a dancing extra. This study was taken for her role in *Lost and Found on a South Sea Island* (1923). A variation on this pose appeared in the January 1923 issue of *Screenland*. Her career ended shortly after the coming of sound.

21 Joan Crawford (Lucille Fay Le Sueur) (1904–1977). A fashion study in a costume from one of her early film roles, as a chorus girl in *Pretty Ladies* (1925), when the ambitious Lucille Fay Le Sueur was still known by her stage name of Billie Cassin. Her leap to fame was spectacular. By 1928 she had become one of MGM's brightest new stars. By 1930 it was clear that she would also be one of its most enduring properties.

22 Jeanne Eagels (1894–1929). A celebrated beauty of the American stage, she became one of the decade's greatest stars by playing Sadie Thompson in Somerset Maugham's *Rain*. She made only five films in her career, but in these created a dazzling impact. This stunning portrait was taken for *Man, Woman and Sin* (1927). Eagels died of drink, drugs and an excess of high living. A film made of her life in 1957 starred Kim Novak.

23 Joan Crawford (1904–1977). A portrait study of the young starlet taken in 1925.

24 Wallace Beery (1885–1949). Beery began his theatrical career at the age of 16 as an assistant to the elephant trainer with the Ringling Brothers' circus. His roles in silent films alternated between heavies and slapstick comedy. When sound was introduced he became a stalwart of MGM until his death and he won an Oscar for his role in *The Champ* (1931). At one time he was married to Gloria Swanson. This study dates from the early twenties.

25 Mae Murray (Marie Adrienne Koenig) (1885–1965) appears here in costume for the climactic ballroom number in MGM's spectacular silent version of Franz Lehar's *Merry Widow* (1925), re-tailored to provide the cinematic apogee of Mae's particular talents. The film became the studio's biggest money-maker for that year. Mae had been a dancer in the Follies and began her film career in 1916. She was one of the most popular, vibrant, and arguably silliest, of the silent stars. Billed as 'the girl with the bee-stung lips', her look was aped by girls everywhere. In life, as on film, she married a charming penniless European prince. Only the film provided a happy ending.

26 Gwen Lee (born 1905) and Tim McCoy (Timothy John Fitzgerald McCoy) (1891–1978) as Betsy Ross and George Washington in a photographic tableau of 'The Making of the First Flag'. Constantly keeping the studio's name in the press of the nation was a large part of the publicity department's function. One part of a contract player's build-up in the public's mind was to dress them up as reincarnations of famous historical figures for a session in the gallery. Such 'page-lighteners' featured women more often than men, and preferably disguised as sirens like Salomé and Cleopatra or heroines famed from literature.

27 Claire Windsor (Clara Viola Cronk) (1897–1972) photographed as Betsy Ross in this re-enactment of the painting, 'The Making of the First Flag', by Alfred Russell. Like plate 26, this study was a studio publicity department's unsolicited contribution to the annual 4th of July celebrations. The idea for this picture came when someone in publicity realized that the lovely blonde, blue-eyed Miss Windsor was Tim McCoy's leading lady in *The Frontiersman* (1926), another of this popular Western and action star's films set in America's Revolutionary past.

28 Greta Garbo (Greta Gustafsson) (born 1905) and John Gilbert (John Pringle) (1895–1936) as Anna Karenina and Vronsky in an on-set shot for *Love* (28 July 1927), in the second of their four films together made at the height of their intermittent affair. The affair whipped the American public into such a frenzy of curiosity that the title of the film based on Tolstoy's novel about the adulterous *Anna Karenina* was changed to *Love*. Tolstoy's son loved the movie.

29 Leatrice Joy (Leatrice Joy Zeidler) (1896–1985). Joy made her film debut in 1915 and was still active on stage and screen in the early 1950s. Leatrice became a major twenties' star when Cecil B. DeMille cast her to replace Gloria Swanson as his conception of a 'frivolous flapper' in films including *Manslaughter* and *Triumph*. Bull had already photographed Leatrice at Goldwyn in the early twenties before taking this photo in 1928. Joy is sporting the bobbed hair style she popularized.

30 Greta Garbo as Anna Karenina in an on-set study taken by Bull during production of *Love* (28 July 1927).

31 Lillian Gish (Lillian de Guiche) (born 1896) in a costume study (5 July 1927) to promote her role in her last silent film, which was also her last film at MGM, *The Wind* (1928). As with Garbo, whose rise at the studio marked the decline of Miss Gish, Lillian's favorite portrait photographer was usually Ruth Harriet Louise.

32 Anna May Wong (Wong Liu Tsong) (1907–1961). The Los Angeles-born Chinese actress of American movies began her film career as an extra in 1919 and made her last film in 1960. In 1928 at the height of her fame she worked in Berlin and London. She starred in several major silent and sound British films, including *Piccadilly* (1929), and co-starred on stage with Laurence Olivier in *Circle of Chalk* (1929). This study was taken while she was making *Across the Pacific* (1927).

33 Tim McCoy (1891–1978) in an off-set study in his costume for *Riders of the Dark* (29 July 1927), one of five Westerns he made that year. As a popular star of a genre in which dialogue was of minimal importance, McCoy moved easily into the sound era and continued to appear in films into the 1950s. The set seen in the mirror and that behind it are from other MGM films currently in production. Spontaneous, unposed shots like this were common until the early 1930s when the producers' association put thumbs down on releasing photographs they felt might destroy the public's illusion about Hollywood. A side-effect of this ruling on the work of studio photographers was that 'unposed' photographs became a rare sight. By the time Robert Capa was sent by *Life* to photograph the stars on the set of *Notorious* (1945), his pictures showing Bergman and Grant between scenes or surrounded by the tools of their trade, were (and still are) regarded as a revolutionary breakthrough in photographing movies.

34 Tim McCoy. A mood study taken of the actor during a break on location for *Wyoming* (22 October 1927). Like Bull, McCoy had grown up in the West. He entered films as a technical adviser on the first great Western epic *The Covered Wagon* (1923) because of his knowledge of American Indians, their dialects, customs and lore.

35 Ann Dvorak (Ann McKim) (1912–1979) and Raquel Torres (Paula Osterman) (1908–1987). Dvorak was a dance instructor and chorus girl in early MGM musicals before she shot to fame in the early 1930s as the incestuous sister in the classic gangster film *Scarface*. Her first husband was the Liverpool-born actor/director Leslie Fenton; she came to Britain with him in the mid-30s, and appeared on the stage and in three British films during World War II before returning to continue her career in Hollywood. The lovely Mexican, Raquel, who made her screen debut as a Polynesian in *White Shadows of the South Seas* (1928) played decorative leading ladies in foreign language versions of early Hollywood talkies, and glamorous comedy foils in films such as *Duck Soup*. In 1934 she went to Britain to appear in *Red Wagon*. This pose on Malibu beach was taken in 1929 when both girls were briefly under contract to MGM.

36 Ralph Forbes (Ralph Taylor) (1902–1951). On the English stage since childhood, the good-looking London-born actor arrived in Hollywood to play one of the brothers in *Beau Geste* (1926). He went on to play a succession of leading male roles to glamorous female stars in silent films, several opposite his American actress wife Ruth Chatterton, and in the 1930s, opposite his British-born actress wife Heather Angel.

37 Conrad Nagel (1897–1970). A popular if unexciting romantic lead in silent films, he made two with Garbo. His mellifluous voice was considered ideal for sound (he made 10 films in 1929), and he also had a long and distinguished career in talkies, mostly as a character actor. He was the co-founder and former president of the Academy of Motion Picture Arts and Sciences and was involved in the creation of the Academy Awards in 1928, the year in which this portrait was taken.

38 Greta Garbo. A portrait session for her last silent film, *The Kiss* and her first portrait gallery session with Bull (27 August 1929). Temperamentally shy and reclusive, and relying for her art on instinct rather than technique, she had become progressively adverse to being photographed for any reason other than her role in a film. Garbo preferred to work with the same film cameraman (William Daniels) and the same still photographers (William Grimes and Milton Brown) as much as possible.

39 Greta Garbo. Hollywood had almost totally converted to 'talkies' by 1929, two years after the advent of sound, and Garbo, along with Lon Chaney (horror) and Charlie Chaplin (comedy), was the only front ranking star still making silent movies. Portraits such as this one (27 August 1929) kept her public patient even while curios-

ity about her voice, and its eventual impact on her future career, was growing to a fever pitch.

40 Greta Garbo as Anna Christie (19 November 1929). While photographs couldn't talk, this was one of the first portraits the public saw of Garbo in costume and mood for her role in the film in which she did, at last, talk. The immobilized early sound cameras made film close-ups of the actors virtually impossible, but the portrait camera suffered from no such problems, and as a result the only close-ups of Garbo as Anna Christie the public ever saw were those made by Clarence. Meanwhile, careers were being shattered all around her; her former leading man and lover, John Gilbert, had already been proclaimed a disaster in his first talkie.

41 Greta Garbo. Another study taken at the time of *The Kiss*. A variation of this image was used for one of the key poster designs (27 August 1929).

42 Buster Keaton (Joseph Francis Keaton) (1895–1966). The great pensive-faced silent clown got his nickname, Buster, from Harry Houdini, who had watched amazed as the six-month-old toddler survived a fall down a flight of stairs. Buster became part of his parents' acrobatic vaudeville act. His silent films are classics. His slide into obscurity began about the time of this photograph (17 December 1930) but he climbed back to international recognition and acclaim before his death. His last role was in the British-made *A Funny Thing Happened on the Way to the Forum* (1966).

43 Edwina Booth (Josephine Constance Woodruff) (born 1909). In this study, taken for the spectacular early talkie, *Trader Horn* (1930). Booth poses in her costume as 'The White Goddess', a Bardot-like savage raised in the jungles of Africa and ruling over a tribe of superstitious natives, until found by two white hunters. The film was shot on location in Africa during which the beautiful young actress contracted a lingering wasting illness which ruined her subsequent career. This portrait study was taken in the wilds of Bull's gallery in Hollywood (2 January 1931).

44 Lupe Velez (Maria Guadeloupe Velez de Villalobos) (1908–1944). A portrait of the lively *petite* Mexican actress in make-up for her role as the tragic little Indian in *The Squaw Man* (March 1931), the third and last version directed by De-Mille of the seminal Western with which he had begun his film career. Lupe, a star in silent films, was married to the screen's most celebrated Tarzan, Johnny Weissmuller.

45 Anita Loos (1891–1981). The celebrated authoress of *Gentlemen Prefer Blondes* was also one of Hollywood's top screen-writers. She began writing for D. W. Griffith in her teens, and at the time of this study (25 June 1932), had been hired to write stories and scripts for the studio's new acquisition, Jean Harlow. The first fruit of this collaboration between the woman who wrote about blondes and the 'blonde' everybody was writing about, was entitled *Red Headed Woman* (1932).

46 Joan Crawford 1904–1977. A 'mirror, mirror on the wall' shot (December 1930), but Crawford's pensive look belies the fact that for her, the future was rosy indeed, for wasn't she the crown-princess of Hollywood, idol and role-model of millions of young women throughout the land? Although Garbo was the acknowledged 'Queen of Drama' and Norma Shearer, married to the boss, starred in the big prestige production, it was generally known that Crawford's films helped pay the studio's rent.

47 Bessie Love (1898–1987). Always a good sport, Bessie, unlike Crawford, had little to cheer about as she posed for 'seasonal art' heralding 1931 since little more than a year after her triumphant talkie debut in *Broadway Melody*, her MGM contract was finished and her Hollywood career virtually wiped out by a spate of silly musicals. (By 1931 she wasn't even at the studio anymore.) A wise woman, Love left Hollywood for England to make a new life and a new career for herself over there.

48 John (1882–1942), Ethel (Edith) (1879–1959) and Lionel (1878–1954) Barrymore (Blythe). Great fanfare greeted the announcement that the three Barrymores, acknowledged as 'The Royal Family of Broadway', were to work together for the first time on the screen, playing, what else, the ill-fated Russian 'royals' in *Rasputin and the Empress* (1932). Bull took the 'official' and 'unofficial' portraits of the three, here, on the lawn of brother John's rented Hollywood home (8 August 1932).

49 Virginia Cherrill (born 1908). A beautiful blonde society girl who shot to fame as Chaplin's leading lady when she played the blind girl in *City Lights* (1930). She was also John Gilbert's leading lady in *Fast Workers* (1933) at MGM. In 1935, after discarding the first of her five husbands (Cary Grant), she left for England to make a few films, see a few shows, and eventually marry the man who would make her the Countess of Jersey. (Anita Loos couldn't have written it better.)

50 Helen Twelvetrees (Helen Marie Jurgens) (1907–1958). The soulful-eyed actress was grandmother to the photographic book publisher Jack Woody, his lavish picture book, *Lost Hollywood*, was dedicated to the actress who had a brief vogue with her Lillian Gish-like charms in early talkies before becoming one of the army of forgotten stars. This study was dated June 1932, while she was making *Is my Face Red?* at MGM.

51 San Simeon, 18 May 1931. At San Simeon did publisher William Randolph Hearst (1863–1951) a mighty pleasure dome decree, filling his castle, which overlooked the Pacific Ocean between Carmel and San Luis Obispo, with antiques, marble statues, tapestries and treasures from around the world, as a fitting setting for his movie star mistress Marion Davies to entertain the world's Great. Bull, who took more pictures of Davies than of any other star except Garbo, shot this photograph for a magazine spread on 'stars and their homes'.

52 Marion Davies (Marion Cecilia Douras) (1897–1961). A genuinely popular comedienne in silent films, her career continued on well into the talkies, but not entirely due to the support of her besotted press-lord lover. She was first spotted by Hearst around 1916, when she was one of the glorified beauties in the Ziegfeld Follies. She made her first film in 1917 and arrived at MGM in 1924, shortly after its founding, but the slightly stuttering star departed ten years later after she failed to get the role of the Victorian poetess Elizabeth Barrett in *The Barretts of Wimpole Street* (1934). The mistress of the house is seen here in a study taken in July 1932 in the gardens of San Simeon.

53 Marie Dressler (Leila Marie Koerber) (1869–1934). At the time of this portrait (June 1932), the Canadian comedienne and early Chaplin leading lady (*Tillie's Punctured Romance*, 1914) had made a stunning comeback from near-eclipse to become MGM's No. 1 female box-office star in the wake of her dramatic performance opposite Garbo in *Anna Christie* (1930) and her Oscar for her tragi-comedy performance later that same year in *Min and Bill*.

54 Jimmy Durante (James Francis Durante) (1893–1980). The popular stage, nightclub and film comedian, and songwriter was known as 'the great Schnozzola' for his large, bulbous nose, in costume for his role opposite Buster Keaton in *Speak Easily* (1932). Durante, whose star at the studio rose as Keaton's sank, continued in films, nightclubs and TV well into the 1970s.

55 Diana Wynyard (Dorothy Isobel Cox) (1906–1964). An elegant, gifted and beautiful British stage and film actress, best remembered as the tormented wife in the British-made *Gaslight* (1940), made her Hollywood debut in *Rasputin and the Empress*. This study was at the time of her role in the light-hearted comedy *Reunion in Vienna* (1933).

56 Leslie Howard (Leslie Stainer) (1893–1943). This British star took up acting as therapy after suffering from shell-shock in World War I, and died when his plane was shot down in World War II by German raiders. Howard was regarded as one of the foremost stage and film stars of the thirties, starring on both sides of the Atlantic in such films as *The Scarlet Pimpernel* (1935), *Romeo and Juliet* (1936), *Gone with the Wind* (1939) and *Intermezzo* (1939). This portrait was taken when he first co-starred with Norma Shearer in *A Free Soul* (1931), the film with which Clark Gable (his rival in *Gone with the Wind*) shot to stardom.

57 Paulette Goddard (Marion Levy) (born 1911). This starlet study was taken on 13 May 1932 when Paulette was still a blonde, making her way in Hollywood as a chorus girl in musicals and feminine foil in comedy shorts. Soon after this photograph she met Charlie Chaplin, who changed her life and her career. Chaplin made her dye her blonde hair brown, taught her all he knew, turned her into a star with two of his classics, *Modern Times* (1936), and *The Great Dictator* (1940), and, for a time, he was her second husband and she was his third wife. Miss Goddard, fabled for her shrewd investments in jewellery and art, subsequently had two more husbands of her own, the actor Burgess Meredith and the German author Erich Maria Remarque.

58 Lillian Bond (born 1910), taken 1931. This London-born starlet and second lead of some memorable thirties films including *The Old Dark House* (1932), and *The Westerner* (1940), arrived in Hollywood in 1926 and retired from films in the mid-fifties.

59 Carole Lombard (Jane Alice Peters) (1908–1942). This archetypal glamour portrait of the blonde Paramount star, the brightest screwball comedienne of her generation, came out of a session (17 October 1934) to publicize her only MGM film, *The Gay Bride* (1934).

60 Marion Davies (1898–1961), photographed in some of the fine feathers for her role as *Blondie of the Follies* (9 July 1932). Davies' role was loosely woven around the life of the sort of Follies showgirl she herself had been, and for which Anita

Loos, who seemed to be handed every script with a blonde either in the title or the film, provided the sort of snappy dialogue Broadway showgirls were famed for.

61 Bing Crosby (Harry Lillis Crosby) (1904–1977). The enormously popular crooner was borrowed from his home studio, Paramount, to appear in the Marion Davies musical *Going Hollywood* (1933) because MGM had no singing stars of their own under contract, and, as Crosby recalled years later, because Miss Davies wanted him. And, what the power behind the power behind the Hearst press wanted, she invariably got.

62 Charles Boyer (1897–1978). This study was taken on 2 February 1931 at the time that the French stage and screen star was making his first foray on Hollywood by starring in French-language versions of American movies and playing small parts in English films opposite American stars like Claudette Colbert and Jean Harlow. Neither his accent nor his roles (Continental lotharios) appealed to the American audience. His popularity as the 'great lover' of the decade only began four years later. When he next appeared at MGM it was as Greta Garbo's co-star in *Conquest* (1937), but perhaps his most celebrated role was that of the romantic petty criminal Pepe La Moko in *Algiers* (1938).

63 W. S. Van Dyke (William S. Van Dyke II) (1889–1943). Known as Woody 'One-Take' Van Dyke for his quick work, he was one of MGM's most successful and versatile directors famed for action films like *Trader Horn* (1931), *Tarzan, The Ape Man* (1932), *The Thin Man* series, and several of the MacDonald-Eddy operettas. This photograph was taken around 1933.

64 Johnny Weissmuller (Peter John Weissmuller) (1904–1984). Weissmuller, the Olympic swimming champion, was launched to fame in his first starring role as novelist Edgar Rice Burroughs' idea of the ultimate English aristocrat in *Tarzan, the Ape Man* (1932). (Tarzan's first words, 'Me Tarzan, you Jane' were supposedly contributed by Ivor Novello.) Weissmuller is shown here rehearsing his rope tricks 14 February 1933 before swinging through the jungle on reinforced vines to find his mate in the next of one of the longest-running series in the history of Hollywood. Weissmuller finally hung up his loincloth in 1948, by which time his English, if not his dialogue, had improved considerably.

65 Robert Montgomery (Henry Montgomery) (1904–1981). He joined MGM in 1929 and was already well on the way to the top when this photo was taken on 2 July 1930. Always a charming and distinguished leading man in romantic and comedy roles, he established himself as a serious dramatic star with his role as the psychotic killer in Emlyn Williams' psychological thriller *Night Must Fall* (1937). An accomplished director as well as actor, he made a number of films in England in the thirties and forties. In the fifties he concentrated on working in television and coached American Presidents such as Eisenhower on how to talk before a TV camera. Montgomery played Armand Duval, the romantic lead in Garbo's *Camille*.

66 Johnny Weissmuller. Clarence and Johnny shared an interest in hunting and often enjoyed going on sporting trips together. Weissmuller, when not posing as Tarzan, was rarely photographed in anything other than swimming gear. This study dates from 26 December 1934.

67 Jean Harlow (Harlean Carpenter) (1911–1937). Bull's first official session with 'the Platinum Blonde' was taken on 20 July 1932 to launch her as the newest star in MGM's heavens. Her first starring role for the studio was in the title role of *Red Headed Woman*, for which she had to wear a red wig.

68 Jean Harlow and Clark Gable (1901–1960) for their roles in *Red Dust* (1932). The production of this movie was temporarily interrupted by the suicide of Harlow's first husband, producer Paul Bern. The film marked the first star-teaming of the two young performers who went on to become one of the hottest box-office combos of the decade. In 1953 Gable re-made *Red Dust* as *Mogambo*, with brunette Ava Gardner taking the Harlow role.

69 Jean Harlow, taken December 1930. More than a year before Harlow signed with MGM, she worked at the studio on loan-out from her discoverer Howard Hughes to play gangsters' molls in two films at her future home studio.

70 Jean Harlow. Harlow was recognized as the decade's tough brash new sex symbol after her appearance in the 1930 aviation spectacle *Hell's Angels*, but MGM, who signed her in 1932, found it wise to emphasize Harlow's other accomplishments, to make her as acceptable to the women in the audience as she was to the *Field and Stream* crowd. The strategy worked (she was one of the most popular box-office stars of the decade), because Harlow, only twenty-one, really was an outgoing, athletic girl, as much at home with golf-clubs and tennis rackets as with

satin slippers and something loose falling down round her shoulders (1932).

71 Norma Shearer (Edith Norma Shearer) (1900–1983) and Gilbert Adrian (1903–1959). A costume fitting in Shearer's studio bungalow (designed by Cedric Gibbons) and watched by Adrian, the brilliantly innovative head of Metro's wardrobe department, who designed all of Miss Shearer's outfits, as well as the wardrobes for almost every one of the studio's top female stars. This fitting was for her role of Nina in MGM's adaptation of Eugene O'Neill's *Strange Interlude* (1932). After Garbo left MGM, Adrian also left to open his own couture establishment and Norma Shearer, though she had no need to, left the same year. With Adrian's departure, the great age of studio glamour and MGM's pre-eminence in the field waned.

72 Clark Gable (1901–1960). Taken before Gable was told to have his irregular teeth capped and his large ears pinned back. Of course the real reason for his dynamic impact on women was evident in his glance, which did not need cosmetic improvement. It was a new and tougher era in America and by the time that he sat for this portrait (30 October 1931) he was already hard at work on his twelfth film that year. Gable's roles had steadily grown in importance ever since he manhandled the super-sophisticated Norma Shearer in *A Free Soul* (1931), and she liked it. Before the year was out he had become Garbo's leading man in *Susan Lennox*.

73 Veree Teasdale (1906–1987). A sophisticated blonde actress specialising in glamorous, bitchy types who created trouble for gullible men, she was photographed on the MGM lot (the studio cafeteria is behind her) for her only film appearance there, as the woman who wrecked Charles Laughton's home and life in *Payment Deferred* (1932). She did most of her other work during this decade at Warner Brothers. Miss Teasdale became the wife of the actor Adolphe Menjou.

74 Adolphe Menjou (1890–1963). The American-born Menjou excelled in playing suave, dapper foreign-accented men of the world, an image born in silent films with his star-making role in Chaplin's *A Woman of Paris* (1923) which even sound, revealing his rapid-firing and impeccably American-accented speech could not dispel. For years he was high on the list of the world's best-dressed men, and was one of Hollywood's most reliable and distinguished character actors long after he ceased to be a star.

75 Walt Disney (1901–1966). A study made in 1933 when Disney, already something of a national hero for creating Mickey Mouse (before he created *Snow White and the Seven Dwarves*), went to MGM to help out with an animated sequence for the studio's all-star *Hollywood Party* (1933). In return, MGM allowed Disney to feature Greta Garbo in one of his Mickey Mouse cartoons.

76 Jackie Cooper (John Cooper) (born 1921), taken in 1931. Still active in the 1980s, as an actor in such films as *Superman* and on TV, as well as a director, in the thirties Jackie was, next to Shirley Temple, the most popular child star in movies, often co-starring with large, gruff, 'lovable' old Wallace Beery in classics including *The Champ* (1931) and a perfect *Treasure Island* (1934). He was nominated for the best actor award for his performance as *Skippy* (1930), directed by his uncle Norman Taurog.

77 Gary Cooper (Frank J. Cooper) (1901–1961). Cooper came from Montana. He received his elementary schooling in England, and after trying to be a newspaper cartoonist with a Los Angeles paper, drifted into a screen career playing lanky, nonchalant cowboys. A sophisticated, worldly, well-travelled man in private, his screen image was built on playing the man of very few words, but with a look that spoke legions, and which, combined with his long, lanky, quint-essentially American good looks, made this two-time Oscar winner one of the most idolized stars in film history. Cooper was under contract to Paramount from 1926 to 1935 but on loan-out to MGM for two films when he posed for this classic (17 April 1934) portrait session, after completing his role in Marion Davies's last film at MGM, a Civil War comedy-romance *Operator 13*.

78 Gary Cooper, taken 17 April 1934. Cooper was one of the best-dressed men in Hollywood, and regularly visited London to have his suits made by Savile Row tailors.

79 Greta Garbo (born 1905), taken 8 July 1931. In *Susan Lennox, her Fall and Rise* Garbo was a hard-worked farm girl raped by her drunken cousins after which she left the farm; went to the big city; met rich men; was kept by them; met Clark Gable; fell in love with him; worried that he would find out about her; he found out about her; he went to rack and ruin; she went to work in a brothel in South America; they met again. Love triumphed over all. Audiences went home convinced it really did. As long as the woman was Greta Garbo and the man was Clark Gable. Portraits such as these set the advance ball rolling.

80 Greta Garbo as Susan Lennox (8 July 1931).

81 William H. Daniels (1895–1970), taken 21 February 1933. What Clarence Sinclair Bull did for Garbo in the portrait gallery, the great William Daniels, one of the foremost cameramen in movies, did for her on screen. From the moment of her arrival in Hollywood when she made *The Torrent* (1925) until *Ninotchka* (1939) Garbo depended on this man as much if not more than on any of her directors or writers. Daniels was equally brilliant at lighting the other women on the lot; he was as adept with colour film as with black and white; his versatility encompassed the *cinéma vérité* style which he helped to make fashionable with his innovative work on films such as *The Naked City* (1948), for which he won his long-due Academy Award. Daniels began as an assistant cameraman with Triangle in 1917 and, after he had made a brilliant reputation photographing most of Erich von Stroheim's early films at Universal, including *Blind Husbands, Foolish Wives* (1921) and *The Merry Widow* (1925), he was brought to MGM in 1924 by Thalberg.

82 Chris. Even more mysterious than the one she doubled for, nothing is known of 'Chris', Greta Garbo's stand-in during the 1930s.

83 Greta Garbo in Mata Hari's elaborate dance costume (19 November 1931). Garbo used to come alone to Bull's gallery, carrying her costumes on her back rather than having a wardrobe person fussing around her. For *Mata Hari* Adrian designed an exotic and heavy wardrobe. Andy Warhol used this photograph as the basis of a screen print in 1983.

84 Greta Garbo for *As You Desire Me* (13 April 1932). After her completion of this Pirandello role Garbo took a long leave of absence. It would be sixteen months before she made her next film. Meanwhile the public had portraits such as this to keep them keen.

85 Greta Garbo for *Inspiration* (12 December 1930).

86 Greta Garbo as *Mata Hari* (19 November 1931). A study of the actress in mood, and sporting the new look created for her role as Mata Hari, the real-life Dutch national, Java-born, exotic dancer and mysterious World War I German spy who was caught and shot. Almost simultaneously, at a rival studio, Josef von Sternberg was making his tale of a fictitious World War I spy with Garbo's only screen rival, Marlene Dietrich. Not to be left out of the firing line, every studio who had an actress with a foreign accent sent them where Garbo had gone, to lie, to love and to die.

87 Greta Garbo as *Susan Lennox* (18 July 1931).

88 Greta Garbo as *Susan Lennox* (18 July 1931). A fashion shot in which Garbo poses like a rather large and languid moth. Though her preferred wardrobe in private ranged from the casual to the scruffy her Adrian-concocted screen wardrobe dominated the fashion scene in the thirties.

89 Greta Garbo. *As You Desire Me* (13 April 1932).

90 Greta Garbo. A portrait study for *Inspiration* (12 December 1930) based on the play *Sappho*, a modern story with Garbo as an artist's model and high-priced call-girl who, like Camille, meets and falls for a young but penniless man. Garbo was then at the peak of her powers, her beauty and popularity.

91 Greta Garbo as Mata Hari (19 November 1931).

92 Boris Karloff (William Henry Pratt) (1887–1969). Astride his (probably authentic) Chinese throne, Karloff is the diabolical Oriental out to conquer the world in Sax Rohmer's *The Mask of Fu Manchu* (24 August 1932). On loan-out from Universal studios (in part exchange for Diana Wynyard and Lillian Bond) the Dulwich-born small-part character actor became a sensational star after his appearance as the monster in *Frankenstein* (1931). After this, Karloff and horror movies were in fashion and other film companies leapt aboard. Even MGM, former home of the late Lon Chaney, the original man of a thousand faces, started to make a few.

93 Cedric Gibbons (1893–1960) and his movie star wife (1930–1941) Dolores del Rio (Lolita Dolores Martinez Asunsolo Lopez Negrette) (1905–1983) posing (28 May 1931) in the Malibu beach-home designed by Gibbons, a celebrated production designer and head of MGM's art department from 1924 until 1958. Gibbons was also the designer of the Oscar statuette, winning the award himself 11 times. Miss del Rio, a star in movies since 1925, was Mexican, and so beautiful that the coming of sound held no serious problems for her. Although she appeared in a couple of films for MGM, she was never under contract to them.

94 MGM art-deco revolving entrance designed by Cedric Gibbons for *Grand Hotel* (30 January 1932).

95 Joan Crawford (1904–1977), taken April 1933. One of the popular 'at-home' series carefully set up to illustrate that a star's duty, to look her best for her public, is an endless one. Getting an even tan was not all pleasure.

96 Joan Crawford. Here, (24 May 1930) this most dedicated of thirties' stars combines a break on

her perfectly evenly mown lawn with more work on her tan and simultaneously replying to her own fan mail. Crawford is happy autographing hundreds of Bull's recent portraits of her. For the almost two decades Crawford was under contract to MGM the studio paid for prints of her pictures and the postage, which, at an average of 5000 requests per month was quite costly. Crawford, who always maintained that she owed her career to her fans, kept up the practice and paid the postage herself in later years when she was no longer under contract and had started to avoid the sun when she found that it wrinkled the skin.

97 Jean Harlow (1911–1937), taken 8 July 1932. A photograph of Harlow in her swimming pool. Considering the chlorine in the water and the peroxide in her platinum hair, one might assume that this was not a pleasure outing.

98 Jean Harlow, taken 24 January 1934. Lying across Cedric Gibbons's winding art deco staircase constructed for Harlow's *The Girl from Missouri*. Judging from this cheerfully contrived study, one could tell that this was not the film's original title. It began filming as *Born to be Kissed*. Before it was even completed, the film was caught up in the storm of moral outrage starting to sweep America. The real moral revolution took a bit longer but meanwhile puritans were regaining lost ground and Hollywood bowed. Sexually explicit films still in production were toned down. Provocative titles had to be changed. At one point MGM, not knowing what to call a 'Harlow' film that wouldn't sound suggestive, planned to release this film as *100% Pure*.

99 Jean Harlow in her studio dressing room (8 July 1932).

100 Madge Evans (1909–1981). The sister of thirties MGM stills and portrait photographer, Tom Evans and a former child star in silent films, Madge Evans was a very charming and intelligent leading lady in 1930s films such as *Dinner at Eight* (1933) and *David Copperfield* (1934), and in the futuristic classic Anglo/German co-production, *The Tunnel* (1935). Madge Evans retired from films by the end of the decade, soon after her marriage to playwright Sidney Kingsley.

101 Mary Carlisle (born 1912), taken February 1933. The blonde leading lady of innocuous 1930s musicals at Paramount reached her peak as Bing Crosby's leading lady in *Double or Nothing* (1937) and *Dr Rhythm* (1938), which also boasted one of the few screen performances of the British comedienne, Beatrice Lillie. Mary also made several films at MGM including *Should Ladies Behave*. She was out of movies by the 1940s, replaced by a new generation of bubbly blondes like Betty Grable, since one had to be very young for her sort of parts. She married well and in the fifties managed the Elizabeth Arden beauty saloon in Hollywood.

102 Gloria Swanson (Gloria Josephine Mae Swenson) (1897–1983). Swanson was the ultimate embodiment of glamour in the 1920s: the highest paid, the most popular, the most married, whose every mood and action was slavishly imitated by impressionable women. By 1934, when she signed with MGM, her career was at a standstill. Irving Thalberg's idea was to re-make one of the shock-hits of the twenties, *Three Weeks*, with Swanson, who had previous experience in Elinor Glyn vehicles, now cast as the ill-fated Balkan Queen. Many dramatic photographs like this (28 February 1934) were taken and Bull at last had his chance to add to the photographic iconography of one of the most brilliantly photographed women of this century.

103 Gloria Swanson (28 September 1934). Seven months after the last session, and with *Three Weeks* no nearer a starting date, Gloria was back in the gallery. Barely 33, Swanson, by now almost 20 years in the public's eye, looks older. From this time onwards Swanson entered a long professional decline. By 1950, almost totally forgotten by new generations of film-goers, she resurfaced triumphantly as silent star Norma Desmond in *Sunset Boulevard* (1950).

104 Tallulah Bankhead (1903–1968). The wild, the wicked, the wonderful star of almost four decades on the British and American stage (from 1923 to 1930 she worked in London where she was the 'toast of the town'), was photographed at MGM (19 August 1932), where she had come to make *Faithless*, her last film until Hitchcock put her in his *Lifeboat* (1944). Miss Bankhead is in the sort of untypically subdued mood she could only sustain long enough for a portrait camera, but if her photographs fail to capture her vixenish charm and the incendiary spirit which made her the prototype of Scarlett O'Hara and Blanche du Bois, at least they explain why Hollywood first signed her in 1930 to be America's answer to Garbo and Dietrich.

105 Constance Bennett (1904–1965). As sophisticated as Paris could make her, and cracker-barrel smart when it came to negotiating a business deal, Constance, loathed by producers, loved by the public, one of the screen's snazziest dressers,

was the eldest of the 'glamorous Bennett girls', sister to Joan, a famed brunette. At the height of her vogue in the early thirties, every studio tried to find a type like her on their lots (and so avoid having to hire Connie and pay her astronomical price). Carole Lombard (see plate 59) and Bette Davis at Warner Brothers were two of the more famous young girls briefly wedged into the Connie mould.

Because the producers resented her – smart girls who knew they were smart and didn't care who else knew it were never very popular with producers; and because Hollywood columnists, in the pockets of producers, considered her 'stuck-up', features about her were often slanted to make her seem cold and mercenary.

With a tongue as crisp as her marcelled waves she scored points with some memorable *bons mots*. Asked why, with the country struggling on the bread line, she haggled with producers for more money when this was such an unfeminine thing to do and it wasn't even as if she could take it with her, Constance, in a riposte worthy of Jane Austen's Miss Elizabeth Bennett, arched one of her precise eyebrows and shot back, "If I can't take it with me, I'm not going to go."

A less charming side to her nature was that Constance Bennett hated to stand still for stills, or even to sit for portraits (which did not make the photographer's lot an easy one) but she had calmed down a bit by the time Bull took this portrait (15 June 1934) for her role as *The Outcast Lady*. The part had originally been played by Garbo in *A Woman of Affairs*. Both versions were based on Michael Arlen's sensational best seller, *The Green Hat*. The book had been so notorious that neither film version dared to use the original title.

106 Lewis Stone (1879–1953). It is hard to believe, looking at this 1931 portrait of this still-only 52-year-old actor, that he was Garbo's co-star more often than any other actor, cast as everything, from her husband, her lover, her best friend, her doctor and finally, her royal conscience in *Queen Christina*. As a screen lover, even in 1920s, classics such as *The Prisoner of Zenda* (1922) and *Scaramouche* (1923), Lewis looked (and acted) like the leading lady's father. (In the 1952 *Scaramouche* re-make he played the father of the man killed by the man he had played in the earlier version.)

107 Otto Kruger (1885–1974). This 1934 portrait was taken of the 49-year-old silver-haired Broadway actor when he first joined MGM. Like Lewis Stone, Otto Kruger, a distant relative of South Africa's President, Ohm Kruger, initially played love interest to stars like Joan Crawford, and romantic kings in British musicals such as *Glamorous Night* (1937). He worked as a character actor in movies until the 1960s.

108 Elizabeth Allan (born 1908). This British film star was signed by MGM in 1933 and featured in decorative costume roles in films such as *David Copperfield* (1934), *Tale of Two Cities* (1936) and *Camille* (1936). In 1938 she returned to Britain and continued working in films, and in the fifties, on television in the popular series, *What's My Line* (1934).

109 Evelyn Laye (Elsie Evelyn Lay) (born 1900). One of the British theatre's most glamorous musical comedy stars, Miss Laye made only two films in Hollywood, one of which, *The Night is Young* (1934) with a score by Sigmund Romberg, was for MGM. In it she introduced the classic 'Softly, as in a morning sunrise'. The American studios never did capture her charm, but Miss Laye was too popular in England, where she continues to work into the late 1980s, to worry about it.

110 Greta Garbo (born 1905), in costume for her role in Somerset Maugham's *The Painted Veil* (12 September 1934).

111 Greta Garbo, 25 October 1933 (see 112).

112 Greta Garbo. A candle-lit study for her celebrated return from Sweden to start a new contract with her studio as *Queen Christina* (25 October 1933). After an almost two-year-long absence from the screen, she returned to become the highest paid (per film) female star in Hollywood. MGM originally intended to co-star her with Laurence Olivier but at the last minute, after having approved him, Garbo changed her mind and, against opposition from the head of the studio, had Olivier replaced with John Gilbert, her leading man in silent films, who had fallen on hard times.

113 Jeanette MacDonald (1901–1965). Bull took this study of the red-headed energetic screen soprano looking unusually pensive on 7 September 1934, a year and two films (including *The Merry Widow* in 1934, the last of her four films directed by Ernst Lubitsch) since she joined MGM, before her third film, the Victor Herbert operetta *Naughty Marietta* (1934) had been released. She had been a likeable performer since making her film debut in Ernst Lubitsch's *The Love Parade* (1930) but her own career had failed to take off. *Naughty Marietta* changed all that: overnight, with her sunny personality, she was drawn to the

nation's heart as one half of one of the most popular musical duos of the decade (the others were the dancers Fred Astaire and Ginger Rogers). She and her baritone co-star Nelson Eddy made eight films together.

114   Loretta Young (Gretchen Michaela Young) (born 1913) in a portrait (5 May 1933) taken while the twenty-year-old star, who made her first screen appearance as a child of four, was on a loan-out to MGM for *Midnight Mary*. In the fifties and early sixties she had one of the first, most successful and longest-running anthology series on television. In 1986, having been retired for more than twenty years, she returned to television to star in *Christmas Eve*, a sentimental film which became one of the highest rated movies that season.

115   Miriam Hopkins (1902–1972). This portrait was made when Miriam Hopkins was on loan-out from Paramount for *The Stranger's Return* (1933), the delectable actress's only film with MGM, before she became one of the period's major stars when she joined Samuel Goldwyn's studio. In 1937 she went to England to star in *Men are not Gods*.

116   Maurice Chevalier (1888–1972). In the first years of sound, it was accepted in Hollywood that all foreign stars were automatically redundant. In 1929, the French music hall star Maurice Chevalier made his American film debut in the inexpensive little musical *Innocents of Paris*. Like Al Jolson before him, another outsize stage talent new to films, Chevalier proved a meteoric hit with the public and for the next five years he had no need to look back. Before his reputation could wane, he returned to continue his successful career in his native France, after first stopping off to make a couple of musicals in London. Bull did the portraits of Chevalier (9 February 1934) when he played Prince Danilo in MGM's lavish re-make of their silent success *The Merry Widow*, teamed (for the fourth and last time) with Jeanette MacDonald. In 1958 Chevalier returned to MGM to star in the musical *Gigi* (see plate 178).

117   Elsa Lanchester (Elizabeth Sullivan) (1902–1986). The South London comedienne and character actress came to Hollywood with her husband Charles Laughton. When he went to star at MGM she joined him and appeared in supporting roles in films like *David Copperfield* (1934) and *Naughty Marietta* (1935), which she managed to make interesting. Her best-known role in films came the same year, at Universal

studio, when she played *The Bride of Frankenstein*. This study dates from 23 May 1934.

118   Charles Laughton (1899–1962). After winning his Oscar for his performance as the king in *The Private Life of Henry VIII* (1933), Laughton returned to Hollywood from England to become the pre-eminent dramatic star of a decade which he would climax with his greatest role as the tragic *Hunchback of Notre-Dame* (1939). This (1 July 1934) study of the actor in his own character was one of the first made after he came to MGM to star as Dr Barrett in *The Barretts of Wimpole Street* (1934).

119   Frank Lloyd (1888–1960). The Scottish director of over 100 films, starting in 1915, went on to secure his reputation as one of Hollywood's most proficient craftsmen by winning Oscars for his direction of epic British subjects such as *The Divine Lady* (1929), a story of Nelson and Emma Hamilton, *Cavalcade* (1933), and *Mutiny on the Bounty* (1935).

120   Charles Laughton in a character study for his role as Captain Bligh whose despotic behaviour led to the *Mutiny on the Bounty* (18 July 1935).

121   William Powell (1892–1984). In the 1920s this suavest of male stars, who began his screen career as Dr Moriarty opposite John Barrymore's *Sherlock Holmes* (1922), went on to play a string of irascible rogues and memorable villains in films like *Beau Geste* (1925) and *The Four Feathers* (1929). With the coming of sound his elegant appearance, smooth nonchalant manner and beguiling mocking voice made him the perfect star in a string of popular detective films in which he played private eyes, Philo Vance and, unforgettably, Nick Charles in *The Thin Man* (1934), opposite Myrna Loy. Both of them became major stars with the first of that long-running husband and wife series, and they made many other films together (1935).

122   Ethel Barrymore (1879–1959). An off-set shot taken of the actress in costume as the last Russian Empress between scenes for her role in *Rasputin and the Empress* (1932).

123   Herbert Marshall (1890–1966). The five-times-married actor lost a leg in World War I but he barely let on as he moved smoothly through a long succession of roles as a suave, sophisticated, romantic foil to some of the screen's legendary beauties, including Marlene Dietrich, Greta Garbo, Katharine Hepburn, Bette Davis, Kay Francis, Miriam Hopkins, Joan Crawford, Norma Shearer, Madeleine Carroll, Constance Bennett, Claudette Colbert, Barbara Stanwyck, and, in

private life, to Gloria Swanson. His first American film role was in Somerset Maugham's *The Letter* (1929), opposite Jeanne Eagels. He also appeared in the 1940 version opposite Bette Davis, and he twice played Somerset Maugham on the screen, in *The Moon and Sixpence* (1943) and *The Razor's Edge* (1946). He remained active on the screen until the year before his death. This elegant study was taken on 2 February 1934.

124 Ray Milland (Reginald Truscott-Jones) (1905–1986). A portrait of the young Welsh-born film star taken in August 1930 shortly after he arrived in Hollywood to work for MGM as a youthful contract player. His wardrobe, if not his roles, improved somewhat when he switched to Paramount in 1933, where he found himself dressed in a tuxedo and put in a niche not unlike that of his handsome fellow country-man Cary Grant. In 1935 Milland's luck turned when he was picked by Claudette Colbert as her leading man. In 1945, after a couple of roles in films written or directed by Billy Wilder, Milland won an Oscar as the alcoholic writer on the skids in *The Lost Weekend*.

125 Benita Hume (1906–1967), taken February 1934. At MGM from 1934, she was an attractive and stylish leading lady in a series of undistinguished films such as *Tarzan Escapes* (1936). She began her career on the British stage at 17, and in films, including *The Constant Nymph* (1928), *High Treason* (1929), and *Jew Suess* (1934). From the age of 19, she worked opposite stars like Ivor Novello. Famed for her sparkling wit, and courted by some of the wittiest men on both sides of the Atlantic (Ivor Novello, George Gershwin), she married Ronald Colman, the shy, reclusive romantic idol, in 1938, and retired from films. After his death, she married the actor George Sanders.

126 Ronald Colman (1891–1958) in costume and character for his role as Sydney Carton (June 1935), the doomed, romantic hero of Dickens's *A Tale of Two Cities*. Colman was one of the small handful of major silent stars whose reputation (like Garbo's), increased with the advent of sound. Born in Richmond, England, he began in films in 1918, but nothing significant happened until 1923, three years after he arrived in America, when Lillian Gish chose him for her leading man in *The White Sister*. His screen roles, as *Beau Geste* (1926), *Bulldog Drummond* (1929), *Raffles* (1930), in the dual role of *The Prisoner of Zenda* (1937), and as Robert Conway in *Lost Horizon* (1937) made him the romantic idol of

three decades of moviegoers. He won his Oscar for one of his last important films, *A Double Life* (1948).

127 Freddie Bartholomew (Frederick Llewellyn) (born 1924), the London-born boy star of Hollywood films, in costume for his role as the young *David Copperfield* (March 1935). He had already appeared in a couple of British films before starting his American career. For the rest of the decade he was one of the most popular child actors, mostly in British-based costume dramas such as *Little Lord Fauntleroy* (1936), *Lloyds of London* (1936), *Captains Courageous* (1937), *Kidnapped* (1938) and *Swiss Family Robinson* (1940).

128 W. C. Fields (William Claude Dukenfield) (1879–1946). The actor, who began his celebrated stage career soon after he ran away from home aged 11 after a fight with his father, is seen here in costume for his role as Mr Micawber in *David Copperfield* (8 November 1934). Fields took over the (for him) untypical dramatic role when Charles Laughton dropped out. It proved to be one of the great comedian's most memorable screen appearances.

129 Myrna Loy (Myrna Williams) (born 1905) and William Powell (1892–1984). The thirties' favourite on-screen husband and wife team after first playing husband and wife detectives Nick and Nora Charles in *The Thin Man* (1934), are back before the cameras in a session for *After the Thin Man* (1936).

130 The Marx Brothers. Composed Metro-Goldwyn-Mayhem (13 September 1935). Something of Groucho's humour can be gleaned from this (possibly apocryphal) incident which occurred during his first days at MGM. Caught in a lift with a woman whose face was hidden behind her large slouch hat and who studiously ignored him, Groucho, who suspected the stranger's identity, lifted the brim just as the gates opened, recognized Garbo and told her, 'Sorry, I thought it was someone I knew', and sprinted out of the lift before the startled Swedish recluse could do the same.

131 The Marx Brothers, Chico (Leonard Marx) (1886–1961), Groucho (Julius Marx) (1890–1977) and Harpo (Adolph Marx) (1888–1964). The Marx Brothers were photographed clowning for publicity and poster art to herald their signing with MGM and their first film there, *A Night at the Opera* (1935). In 1929 the (originally four) brothers made their first film *The Cocoanuts* (based on one of their stage hits). Their following four films for Paramount also featured the

fourth brother, Zeppo (Herbert Marx) (1901–1979). Bored being the straight man to a team of loonies, he left to become a successful agent. The brothers' anarchic, almost surrealistic absurd outrageous slapstick films attracted a cult following, but cults were not enough to keep movie houses open during the depression. One of their highbrow admirers was MGM's Irving Thalberg who brought the three boys to Culver City and a larger paying public. Purists prefer the films the brothers made at Paramount to their Metro mayhems but everybody preferred the great Margaret Dumont as their regal stooge.

132 A bevy of the famed Albertina Rasch dancers, the hardest worked chorus girls in movies, photographed during a rehearsal break (29 March 1935) for one of the spectacular numbers for the first of the *Broadway Melody* series with which MGM launched their official re-entry into the dance-musical genre. The studio's late entry into this quintessential genres of the decade, had been hampered by their lack of a great dancing star.

133 Eleanor Powell (1912–1982). It wasn't that there were no great dancers in movies or on Broadway, but great dancers with personalities who would fire the public's imagination like Fred Astaire were lacking. With MGM's signing of the brilliant young Broadway tap-dancer Eleanor Powell, their worries were over. Like a neon-lit Peter Pan, here in one of her trademark tuxedo costumes for *Broadway Melody of 1936* (24 June 1935) she soared above the heads of her co-stars and some of the biggest sets ever built for a non-historical MGM movie.

134 Deanna Durbin (Edna Mae Durbin) (born 1921). The mid-thirties was the era of meteoric musical stars who became famous overnight and saved failing studios. Shirley Temple did it for Fox and Deanna Durbin did it shortly after this photo was taken at MGM (3 April 1936) for the ailing Universal studio. This was not due to kindness on the part of MGM but to the studio's short-sightedness. They allowed the teenage soprano to go after she had appeared in only a two-reel musical short for them, *Every Sunday* (1936). Realizing their mistake, they quickly signed up the other girl in that film, Judy Garland.

135 Judy Garland (Frances Gumm) (1922–1969). Like Durbin, Garland made her screen debut in *Every Sunday* (1936). Looking far younger than her nearly 14 years, this portrait is probably the only real childhood the legendary singing star, who began her career on a vaudeville stage at three, ever had.

136 Greta Garbo. In 1936 colour came to Hollywood in a big way and was as big a worry as the introduction of sound had been. This study for *Camille* (1936) was something of a concession to Bull on Garbo's part, as posing for colour portraits was hot, arduous and unrewarding and she needn't have done it. It was a great day when this, albeit rather nondescript, colour portrait of Garbo in the curls and costume of the ill-fated Marguerite Gautier in *Camille* was unveiled. At least everyone now knew that her hair was a kind of blonde and her eyes some sort of blue.

137 Greta Garbo for *Camille* (1936). About this time Bull's position in the gallery had become shaky since younger photographers wanted his spot, and the publicity department was contemplating 'promoting' Clarence out of the MGM portrait gallery altogether. It was then that Garbo, though by now she was making only one film every eighteen months, point blank refused to be photographed by anyone else. Since she was virtually the world-wide symbol of the MGM glamour, what Garbo wanted, she would get, and Bull was allowed to stay in his gallery. His black-and-white portraits of Garbo for *Camille* were some of his finest.

138 Jean Harlow (1911–1937) and Clark Gable (1901–1960). Poster art for *Saratoga* which would prove to be their last teaming in the photographic gallery or on film, in their roles as wise-cracking lovers in the romantic race-track comedy. This, and the following study were taken on 27 May 1937. At the time there were still a few uncompleted scenes on the film. Gallery work usually came after all the work on the film had been completed. Gable and Harlow came in earlier as a favour to Bull, to allow him to take off earlier for his fishing trip. Two weeks later, Harlow was dead. These were among her last portrait sittings.

139 Jean Harlow and Clark Gable, for *Saratoga* (1937).

140 Luise Rainer (born 1910). The Viennese actress, a student of Max Reinhardt, arrived in Hollywood in 1935, replacing Myrna Loy opposite William Powell on *Escapade* (1935) and was hailed as a second Garbo. She won the Oscar two years running for her tearful wifely roles as Anna Held (again opposite William Powell) in *The Great Ziegfeld* (1936), and as long-suffering O-Lan in *The Good Earth* (1937), based on the Pearl S. Buck novel for which this study was made in 1936. Rainer's vogue was effectively over by 1938.

141 Eleanor Powell (1910−1982), in her role as a Hawaiian dancer in *Honolulu* (1939). Having photographed her every which way dancing, it was time to show what her hands could do. In the movie Eleanor not only danced the hula, but several spectacular tap routines aboard a ship.

142 Greta Garbo, in costume as Maria Walewska, Napoleon's Polish mistress, in the epic *Conquest* (1937). Garbo was 32 and when she told Napoleon, "Sire, you stand in the sun", it seemed as if she were talking about herself.

143 Greta Garbo as Maria Walewska for *Conquest* (2 September 1937).

144 Robert Taylor (Spangler Arlington Brugh) (1911−1969) and Hedy Lamarr (Hedwig Kiesler) (born 1915), a study for *Lady of the Tropics* (26 April 1939). When the tall, dark and very handsome romantic idol Robert Taylor played Armand to Garbo's *Camille*, snide critics accused him of being more beautiful than his leading lady. This was impossible when he was cast opposite Hedy Lamarr, in this, her first film for the studio.

145 Hedy Lamarr. When she was still in her teens, Max Reinhardt declared the young Viennese actress to be "the most beautiful girl in Europe". She entered films and gained world-wide notoriety by appearing nude in a Czech-made film, *Extase* (1933). By 1937, when MGM's Louis B. Mayer spotted her on one of his talent-scouting safaris to Europe, she was single and on her way to Hollywood, where she was billed as the world's most beautiful woman. She made a sensation in her first American film playing a rich European tourist shimmering with diamonds and flirting with danger in *Algiers* (1938).

146 Hedy Lamarr, another study made in 1938.

147 Greta Garbo in a study as *Ninotchka* (9 August 1939). Garbo needed a hit. Ernst Lubitsch joined MGM to direct her in a cold-war comedy set in Paris, with Garbo as Russian envoy extraordinaire, Comrade Ninotchka. The film was her first popular success for more than seven years.

148 Jeanette MacDonald (1902/3−1965) and Nelson Eddy (1901−1967) the screen's singing sweethearts in costume for their characters in Noel Coward's *Bitter Sweet* (1940).

149 Hedy Lamarr, photographed in a 1939 fashion session wearing a dress by Adrian.

150 Clark Gable as Rhett Butler and Vivien Leigh (Vivien Hartley) (1913−1967) as Scarlett O'Hara promoting *Gone With The Wind* (28 June 1939). This was the most eagerly awaited film of the decade, perhaps of all time. The American public had made Gable's casting a foregone conclusion almost from the moment it was known the screen rights had been bought. These portraits with him and his leading lady, the little-known (to American audiences) British actress Vivien Leigh were their first good chance to see the girl who had been chosen to play Scarlett. She went on to win the first of her two Oscars playing southern belles. The costumes for the film were designed by Walter Plunkett.

151 Clark Gable as Rhett Butler in *Gone With The Wind*.

152 Clark Gable and Vivien Leigh for *Gone With The Wind* (1939).

153 Katharine Hepburn (born 1909). With her first official MGM portrait session on 17 August 1940 in connection with her role in *The Philadelphia Story*, she found a photographer with whom she could work well: during her next seven years at Metro Bull took portraits that satisfied even the most demanding critics – the publicity department, the fans, and the star herself. Hepburn was a great photogenic subject. During her previous years in Hollywood, under contract to RKO studios where her regular portrait photographer was the great Ernest A. Bachrach, she made herself available to some of the best photographers of the day, among them Munkasci, Hoyningen-Huene, Horst and Beaton. This timeless portrait was one of many taken in the costume and hairstyle for her role as the glittering ice-maiden Tracy Lord whose defrostation was the theme of *The Philadelphia Story*.

154 Eleanor Powell (1912−1982) and Fred Astaire (Frederick Austerlitz) (1899−1987) in the celebrated tap dance routine for the 'Begin the Beguine' number in *Broadway Melody of 1940* (21 September 1939). This film was the one and only teaming of the screen's two greatest hoofers in the last of the series of lavish musical revues.

155 Harry James (1916−1983). James began his career at the age of four as 'the human eel' in a contortionist act, but became famous as a trumpet player and leader of one of the most popular big bands of the forties. He appeared with his band in several war-time musicals including *Best Foot Forward* (1943).

156 Katharine Hepburn. A generic study made at the time she was making *Woman of the Year* (27 October 1941). In this film Hepburn teamed for the first time with Spencer Tracy and consolidated her triumph in *The Philadelphia Story* the previous year.

157 Cary Grant (Alexander Archibald Leach) (1904−

1986). This Bristol-born tight-rope walker ran away from home at 13 and went on to be one of the American cinema's legendary stars for over 40 years. This study was taken by Bull at the time of Grant's performance opposite Hepburn in *The Philadelphia Story* (9 August 1940).

158 Judy Garland. As a young impressionable teenager working with, and one time even co-starring in the same film (*Ziegfeld Girl*, 1941) with two of the most glamorous women in Hollywood, Lana Turner and Hedy Lamarr, Garland, already more popular at the box-office than either of the other two, nevertheless felt 'unglamorous'. For her coming-of-age role in *Presenting Lily Mars* (9 November 1943) Bull made her beautiful. All magazines had converted to full-colour printing by the 1940s and like most major portrait sessions of the period, this picture was also taken in colour.

159 Peter Lorre (Laszlo Loewenstein) (1904–1964). Character study taken of his role in *They Met In Bombay* (1941), in which the bulging-eyed Hungarian actor was once again cast as a slant-eyed oriental. Lorre had been an international sensation as the psychopathic child-murderer in the German film M (1931) before he came to Hollywood, via England, where he made two films with Alfred Hitchcock, *The Man Who Knew Too Much* (1934), and *The Secret Agent* (1936). In America, as well as acting in films like *The Maltese Falcon* (1941) and *Casablanca* (1942), he starred in a string of detective thrillers as the soft spoken, ju-jitsu-skilled hero who always got the criminal, Mr Moto.

160 Hedy Lamarr (born 1915). Out of the thousands of photographs taken of her throughout her career, and the hundreds of portraits Bull shot of the exotic Austrian in her seven years with MGM, this (8 August 1940) was her own favourite, and she selected it for use on the cover of her torrid autobiography, *Ecstasy & Me* (1966).

161 Katharine Hepburn (born 1909). This generic portrait of the actress (13 August 1944) was taken for *Without Love*, her third film with Spencer Tracy adapted from another stage play written for her by Philip Barry, the author of her earlier successes *Holiday* and *The Philadelphia Story*.

162 Edmund Gwenn (1875–1959). The Welsh-born character actor and Pal, the American male collie (1940–1954) re-creating one of the dramatic highlights from *Lassie Come Home* (1943). Gwenn had already had an enormously successful career as a character actor on both sides of the Atlantic, and went on to win the supporting Oscar for his role as Santa Claus in *Miracle on 34th Street* (1947). Pal's performance as the loyal British bitch had the critics singing his praises, one of them even going so far as to compare him to the studio's resident dramatic actress by describing him as a 'Greer Garson in furs'.

163 Pal (1940–1954). Another study of the intelligent and good-looking collie who, like the studio's other stars, had to do his share of posing in the gallery, in this case for Christmas greetings to dogs and their owners around the world. Pal originally won the coveted female lead (a deception no one spotted at the time) over more than 300 other candidates for the star-making role of the British 'heroine' of Eric Knight's classic children's novel. There were six sequels, a 1947 radio series (for which Pal did his own barking), and a long running TV series. Pal only appeared in the first few films, but six generations of his male descendants helped to keep the part in the family.

164 Spencer Tracy (1900–1967) and Katharine Hepburn. 'Twas the time before Christmas (7 December 1949), and the studio needed some new shots of these popular stars, already on their way to becoming a Hollywood legend, to promote their third film together, *Without Love* (1945). Tracy hated being photographed but loved Miss Hepburn which shows in the picture, and allowed her to coax him into Bull's gallery for sessions such as this which captured their humorous adoration of one another.

165 Lana Turner (Julia Jean Mildred Frances Turner) (born 1920) and Clark Gable in a deliberately suggestive two-shot to herald their first teaming as the screen's newest romantic pairing, in *Honky Tonk* (1941). As Gable's leading lady, Turner officially graduated to MGM's top rank and was promoted by them as the successor to the late Jean Harlow. Bull, who had so often photographed Gable and Harlow together in the thirties, was trying to recapture that mood.

166 Greta Garbo (born 1905). A photograph from the thirty-six-year-old Garbo's last studio portrait session (3 October 1941) and one of her few colour portraits, in the contemporary look she had for her last film playing all-American twins in *Two Faced Woman* (1941). After the film's failure Miss Garbo took a break from filming until a more suitable role for her talents could be found but apart from a 1949 screen test, she never appeared in another film.

167 Cyd Charisse (Tula Ellice Finklea) (born 1921).

A ballet dancer from the age of 13, she broke into movies in 1943 with the name of Lily Norwood. By 1945 she had been featured in films like *Ziegfeld Follies* and was being built up by MGM as one of their most decorative stars, as can be seen by this 1947 colour study. But not until the start of the next decade, as partner to the studio's great musical male dancers, Gene Kelly (*Singing in the Rain*, 1952) and Fred Astaire (*The Bandwagon*, 1953) and other musicals of that era, did her long-legged talent glide into its own and elevate her to one of the glories of the decade.

168 Lana Turner. Newly a mother of little Cheryl (who would make her own headlines one day), and freshly divorced from the father (Steve Crane), Lana's return to the screen was treated as a major event. Though her usual photographer by then was Bull's former assistant, Eric Carpenter, he was at war and it was Bull's assignment to show that motherhood had not dulled her sex-appeal but had only made her blossom more (28 October 1943).

169 Ava Gardner (born 1922). By 1947, when this portrait was taken, Ava Gardner, after spending the previous six years working her way up through bits in shorts, as chorus girls in musicals, in walk-ons and small parts in features, leads in B films and in films made on loan-outs to other studios, and getting more publicity from her short first marriage to Mickey Rooney than all these films put together, had arrived in her own right. After her vibrant performances in *The Killers* (1946) and *The Hucksters* (1947), she was recognized as one of MGM's greatest assets: one of the most beautiful women in America and one of the most popular sex symbols with male and female fans.

170 Robert Mitchum (born 1917). Mitchum made his film debut at RKO in 1943 and in his first year, due in part to Hollywood's shortage of presentable men, rapidly rose from playing extras and bits to playing marines, GIs, combat pilots, small-time hoods and Wild-West rustlers in at least 18 films. His career took off properly with *The Story of GI Joe* (1945). The following year he made his first film at the prestigious MGM as the sympathetic good guy opposite Katharine Hepburn in *Undercurrent* (1946), one of that studio's first forays into the increasingly popular 'film noir' genre in which Mitchum would define his image and secure his popularity back at RKO.

171 Elizabeth Taylor (born 1932). Born in London of American parents, her family returned to the USA shortly before the outbreak of World War

II. She was 10 when she made her film debut in 1942 at Universal studios in *There's One Born Every Minute*. Her next film, *Lassie Come Home* (1943), was for MGM, where she remained for the next 19 years, finally leaving after winning her first Oscar for the film she did not want to make, *Butterfield 8* (1960). She was just 16, and just about to start dating Howard Hughes, when Bull took this, his first colour portrait of her in 1948 to announce her 'coming of age' as one of the studio's leading female stars.

172 Marlene Dietrich (Maria Magdalena von Losch) (born 1901). At Paramount in the thirties Dietrich had been one of the decade's towering stars, shaped by her mentor, Josef von Sternberg, to be 'his' Garbo: as mysterious, as beautiful and as solitary. All of which she duly became for him. On the dissolution of their partnership, her career began to flounder. She started to freelance. She was named box-office poison and her studio paid her not to make her last film in 1937. In search of a new and less decadent image than the one which only von Sternberg knew how to control and employ, she posed for different photographers. Portraits are cheaper than films. It was about this time that she went to Bull as a private client. Bull's photos are of a woman who used mystery as an alluring smoke screen but little else and who had the strength needed to adapt, survive and come back. Soon after this portrait was taken she appeared with renewed success as the Wild-West saloon singer Frenchie in *Destry Rides Again* (1939). Her career on screen, stage and records continued well into the 1970s. Bull subsequently photographed her when she came to make her only film at MGM, a slice of oriental hokum called *Kismet* (1943).

173 Ava Gardner. Gardner was North Carolina's most celebrated daughter who had first come to Hollywood's attention when a studio talent scout saw a photo taken of her by her brother-in-law. In this study, taken on 27 May 1947, shortly after she divorced her second husband, musician Artie Shaw (formerly married to Lana Turner), it is hard to believe looking at this physical embodiment of all that is luxe, *volupté* and charm, that she was one of six children of a poor tenant farmer who helped to pick bales of cotton in her childhood.

174 Joan Greenwood (1921–1987). This enchanting husky-voiced, petite blonde leading lady of four decades of British films starred with equal success on stage and screen and remains unforgettable as Gwendolen in *The Importance of Being Earnest*

(1952) and for her participation in a series of classic British comedies starring Alec Guinness including *Kind Hearts and Coronets* (1949) and *The Man in the White Suit* (1950). Bull took this photograph of her at the time of her only Hollywood-made film *Moonfleet* (1954).

175 Lucille Ball (1911–1989). The flaming redheaded daughter of a mining engineer and a concert pianist had already been working on screen a dozen years at RKO when she arrived at MGM in 1943. A war-time pin-up favourite, Bull's photograph is a GI's idea of a chorus girl's portrait, which was pretty much what she played in MGM musicals such as *Dubarry was a Lady* (1943) and *Meet the People* (1944). Her real success and the reason for her enduring fame came ten years after this photograph when she starred in *I Love Lucy*, one of American TV's longest running and funniest comedy series.

176 Angela Lansbury (born 1925). The granddaughter of the Labour Party leader George Lansbury, she moved to Hollywood from England in 1944, and was nominated for an Oscar as best supporting actress for her first role in *Gaslight* (1944). Lansbury has been honoured with awards for her work on stage, screen and television ever since. In this 1947 portrait Bull tried to give a rather cute no-nonsense English girl a look of Hollywood sultriness and sexiness.

177 Maria Schell (Margarete Schell) (born 1926). For a time in the fifties the Viennese older sister of actor Maximilian Schell was regarded as the pre-eminent European actress of her generation, noted for roles which demonstrated her capacity to suffer exquisitely. She won the 1954 Cannes film festival award for her performance in *Die Letzte Brücke (The Last Bridge)*, and the 1956 Venice festival award for her role in *Gervaise* (1955). On the wave of her European fame she was brought to Hollywood to make her debut as Grushinskaya, the heroine of Dostoevsky's *The Brothers Karamazov* (1958), a role that was much talked about because of Marilyn Monroe's expressed desire to play it. Bull's portraits of Schell, which deliberately echo his huge close-up portraits of Garbo in the 1930s, did their share to peak the public's curiosity about this enigmatically-smiling tearful actress.

178 Louis Jourdan (Louis Gendre) (born 1919), Leslie Caron and Maurice Chevalier in costume for *Gigi* (1958). Along with his later portraits of Maria Schell, *Gigi* was one of Bull's last major photographic sessions before he retired. This delightful musical adaptation of Colette's classic short story was one of the last great triumphs of the MGM studio style. As well as winning eight Oscars, the film restored the American career of the legendary French music hall entertainer Maurice Chevalier, whom Bull had first photographed (see plate 116) when he went to MGM in 1934 to play Prince Danilo in *The Merry Widow*.

179 Leslie Caron (born 1931). The Parisian ballerina turned actress was discovered for films and brought to America by Gene Kelly to be his leading lady in *An American in Paris* (1951). Miss Caron was a gamine very much in the Audrey Hepburn mould: Caron received the role in *Gigi* when Hepburn was not available for the film, and she made her London stage debut as *Ondine* (also an original Hepburn role). She followed her film debut with the title roles in *Lili* (1953), *Gaby* (1956), *Gigi* (1958) and *Fanny* (1961). Her second husband (1956–1966) was the British theatrical director Sir Peter Hall. This study was made in 1953.

180 Claire Bloom (born 1931). This London-born actress appeared on stage in her teens and was a famous Ophelia – her withdrawn aloofness in this role is suggested by this 1958 portrait. She made her film debut in *The Blind Goddess* (1948) but achieved world fame as Chaplin's leading lady in *Limelight* (1952). Her first Hollywood film, and the occasion for this study, was *The Brothers Karamazov* (1958).

181 Shirley MacLaine (Shirley Maclean Beatty) (born 1934). This actress, authoress and activist, sister of Warren Beatty, was originally a dancer in the chorus of a Broadway musical. She entered movies in 1955 after being spotted by a Hollywood producer the night she replaced the star who had broken her leg. Through the 1950s, before she teamed up with director Billy Wilder and actor Jack Lemmon, she found a niche for herself as a kooky hooker with heart of gold. She was one of the last stars Bull photographed at MGM.

182 Grace Kelly in a portrait study taken for her interpretation of the aloof Tracy Lord opposite Bing Crosby and Frank Sinatra in *High Society* (1956), MGM's musical version of *The Philadelphia Story*.

183 Grace Kelly (1929–1982). The niece of Pulitzer-Prize winning playwright, George (*Craig's Wife*) Kelly. Kelly made her film debut in *Fourteen Hours* (1951) and she won her Oscar playing the embittered wife in *The Country Girl* (1954). Best remembered for her role as a cool, blonde, patri-

cian leading lady in three movies made by Alfred Hitchcock she retired from films to marry a prince and become Her Serene Highness, Princess Grace of Monaco. This, one of her last film portraits before her marriage, was taken when she was cast as a sheltered Princess discovering love in *The Swan* (1956).

Selected Bibliography

Books

James Abbé, *Stars of the Twenties*, 1975 (text by Mary Dawn Earley).

Robert Brindan, *De Meyer*, 1976 (with a biographical essay by Philippe Jullian).

Clarence Sinclair Bull and Raymond Lee, *Faces of Hollywood*, 1968.

Gary Carey, *All the Stars in Heaven – the Story of Louis B. Mayer and MGM*, 1981.

Michael Conway, *The Films of Greta Garbo*, 1968.

Raymond Durgnat and John Kobal, *Greta Garbo*, 1968.

John Douglas Eames, *The MGM Story*, 1982.

John Engstead, *Star Shots*, 1978.

Allen Eyles, David Fahey and Linda Rich, *That was Hollywood – the 1930s*, 1987.

David Fahey and Linda Rich, *Masters of Starlight: Photographers in Hollywood*, 1988.

Joel W. Finler, *The Hollywood Story*, 1988.

Roman Freulich, *Forty Years in Hollywood: Portraits of a Golden Age*, 1971.

Arnold Genthe, *As I Remember*, 1937.

Leslie Halliwell, *Halliwell's Filmgoers Companion*, 1984 (Eighth Edition).

George Hurrell, *The Hurrell Style*, 1977.

Ephraim Katz, *The International Film Encyclopaedia*, 1980.

John Kobal, *Hollywood Glamor Portraits 1926–1949*, 1976.

John Kobal, *Movie Star Portraits of the Forties*, 1977.

John Kobal, *The Art of the Great Hollywood Portrait Photographers*, 1980.

John Kobal, *Hollywood Color Portraits*, 1981.

Bert Longworth, *Hold Still Hollywood*, 1937.

Frederick Sands and Sven Broman, *The Divine Garbo*, 1979.

Klaus-Jürgen Sembach, *Greta Garbo Portraits 1920–51*, 1985.

Paul Trent and Richard Lawton, *The Image Makers*, 1972.

Paul Trent and Richard Lawton, *Grand Illusions*, 1973.

Mark A. Vierira, *Hollywood Portraits: Classic Scene Stills 1929–41*, 1988.

Alexander Walker, *Garbo: A Portrait*, 1982.

Jack Woody, *Lost Hollywood*, 1988.

Articles

Clarence Sinclair Bull, 'Let There Be Flashlight', *Popular Photography*, August 1937.

Clarence Sinclair Bull, 'Why I build Gadgets', *Popular Photography*, January 1940.

Clarence Sinclair Bull, 'Glamor through Simplicity', *Prize Photography*, vol. VI, no. 2, 1941, pp. 8, 9, 51.

Clarence Sinclair Bull, 'How I make my color photographs', *The Ansconian*, July-August 1945.

Clarence Sinclair Bull, 'Stars in my Lens – Jean Harlow', *Rangefinder*, July 1963.

Clarence Sinclair Bull, 'Stars in my Lens – Greta Garbo', *Rangefinder*, August 1963.

Teet Carle, 'Rembrandts with Shutters', *Image*, vol. III, no. 1, February 1968.

Joseph Stillman, 'The Stills Move the Movies', *American Cinematographer*, November 1927, pp. 7–8.

Inez Wallace, 'Shooting Stars in Hollywood' (interview with Clarence Sinclair Bull), *Cleveland Plain Dealer*, 4 October 1936.

'Montana Parade', *Great Falls Tribune*, 22 November 1964, cover, pp. 2 & 5.

'The Old Black and White Magic – Hurrell inspires the Rising Star Photographers', *Vanity Fair*, August 1985, p. 35.

Index of Plates

(References are to plate numbers)

Photograph of Louis B. Mayer and 64 MGM stars for the Studio's 20th birthday, 1943

Left to right,
Front row:

James Stewart, Margaret Sullavan, Lucille Ball, Hedy Lamarr, Katharine Hepburn, Louis B. Mayer, Greer Garson, Irene Dunne, Susan Peters, Ginny Simms, Lionel Barrymore.

Second row:

Harry James, Brian Donlevy, Red Skelton, Mickey Rooney, William Powell, Wallace Beery, Spencer Tracy, Walter Pidgeon, Robert Taylor, Pierre Aumont, Lewis Stone, Gene Kelly, Jackie Jenkins.

Third row:

Tommy Dorsey, George Murphy, Jean Rogers, James Craig, Donna Reed, Van Johnson, Fay Bainter, Marsha Hunt, Ruth Hussey, Marjorie Main, Robert Benchley.

Fourth row:

Dame May Whitty, Reginald Owen, Keenan Wynn, Diana Lewis, Marilyn Maxwell, Esther Williams, Ann Richards, Martha Linden, Lee Bowman, Richard Carlson, Mary Astor.

Fifth row:

Blanche Ring, Sara Haden, Fay Holden, Bert Lahr, Frances Gifford, June Allyson, Richard Whorf, Frances Rafferty, Spring Byington, Connie Gilchrist, Gladys Cooper.

Sixth row:

Ben Blue, Chill Wills, Keye Luke, Barry Nelson, Desi Arnaz, Henry O'Neill, Bob Crosby, Rags Ragland.